This Journal Belongs to

_____

_____

DO NOT FEAR: I am with you;
do not be anxious:
I AM YOUR GOD.
I WILL STRENGTHEN YOU,
I WILL HELP YOU,
I WILL UPHOLD YOU
with my victorious right hand.

ISAIAH 41:10

"Working together to create this lovely guided journal, Debra Kelsey-Davis and Kelly Johnson have brought their extensive personal experiences caring for loved ones to bear to help others find peace in their caregiving journeys."

Amy Goyer
Author of *Juggling Life, Work, and Caregiving*

"In *The Caregiver's Companion*, the authors provide a supportive, insightful, and practical guide for anyone engaged with caregiving. This valuable spiritual resource resonates with wisdom and compassion gained by those who have experienced the hills and valleys of caregivers."

Joyce Rupp
Author of *Praying Our Goodbyes*

"This terrific new Catholic resource brightens the day for anyone lost in the busyness of caring for a loved one. If you'd love a well-deserved pat on the back and some soothing balm for your careworn soul, *The Caregiver's Companion* is for you!"

M. Donna MacLeod
Author of the Seasons of Hope series

"When you're serving as a caregiver for a loved one, life can feel overwhelming. Debra Kelsey-Davis and Kelly Johnson have created a beautiful gift that reminds those of us who care for our loved ones that we are never alone in this journey. *The Caregivers Companion* is an interactive tool to accompany and support caregivers through the challenges we face and to remind us to savor the blessings as well. It's exactly what I need to help me accompany my parents with generosity, trust, and faith!"

Lisa M. Hendey
Author of *The Grace of Yes*

"Caregiving can sometimes feel like a cloud that never leaves you, a twilight world that is neither night nor day. *The Caregivers Companion* journal will help you get—and keep—your bearings. It will help convert the ongoing task of caregiving from drudgery to loving encounter. By covering all the key elements that caregivers need to reflect on and work through, this journal will begin as a companion and become a keepsake."

Jim Healy
Author, speaker, and president of Rooted in Love

The Caregiver's Companion

A Christ-Centered Journal to Nourish Your Soul

Debra Kelsey-Davis and Kelly Johnson

Founders of Nourish for Caregivers

AVE MARIA PRESS AVE Notre Dame, Indiana

Founded in 1865, Ave Maria Press is a ministry of the United States Province of Holy Cross.

www.avemariapress.com

Paperback: ISBN-13 978-1-59471-916-5

Cover image "Blue and Gold Birch Trees" painting © 2019 by Betsy O'Neill, www.betsyoneillfineart.com.

Cover design by Katherine Robinson.

Interior design by Kristen Hornyak Bonelli and Katherine Robinson.

Printed and bound in the United States of America.

Contents

A NOTE FOR YOU BEFORE WE BEGIN

FROM THE AUTHORS OF *The Caregiver's Companion*

Caregiving may very well be one of the most challenging times in anyone's life. Yet caregiving is also a time filled with some of life's most precious blessings. We know; we've been there.

Our passion for creating this guided journal came from our own personal caregiving experiences. We know that, without faith, we would never have been able to see our blessings or learn how to accept and embrace our circumstances. Knowing Jesus and trusting God has provided a bedrock of sustaining graces and moments of joy. And we want the same for you.

Caregiving is often an unexpected and an ever-changing journey. Some days can be mind-numbingly boring, others extremely painful, and others warm us with glimpses of memories past. Sometimes we put our head down and plow ahead. Other times we're so blinded and dazed we cannot focus on even the simplest of tasks. Doubts and unresolved issues wait in the wings, ready to take center stage. But take heart: You are not defined by those problems, concerns, and fears. You are to shine, to be "light" and "salt" to those for whom you care (see Matthew 5:13–16): you are called to be Christ to them in ways God has prepared you to be. Listen as the Lord speaks to your heart:

> For I know well the plans I have in mind for you . . . plans for your welfare and not for woe, so as to give you a future of hope. When you call me, and come and

pray to me, I will listen to you. When you look for me, you will find me. Yes, when you seek me with all your heart, I will let you find me . . . and I will change your lot. (Jer 29:11–14)

Kelly's story: Every caregiver's story is unique. For me, life abruptly changed with a cancer diagnosis; my then-five-year-old son, Bobby, had a brain tumor. One day was filled with executive meetings and presentations; the next with three ambulance rides and tremendous worry and uncertainty. Surgery, chemotherapy, and radiation made for years of long nights. My husband, Bob, and I remain amazed at the beautiful graces we received from this journey. Plus, the story is a happy one, as Bobby is now in college with ongoing support and caring.

Deb's story: Caregiving triggered a collision course between my career and my faith, causing me to leave the corporate world to care for my mother-in-law, Eva, in our home as she battled and lost her fight with cancer. Though I am a registered nurse, I was not prepared for the emotional crises and spiritual isolation that came with caregiving.

Certain that many others have similar struggles, we felt called to start a ministry in our church. Searching for Christ-centered programs and materials, we found none. So, we created Nourish for Caregivers, grounded in our Catholic faith and focused on the practical, emotional, and spiritual needs of family caregivers. Nourish for Caregivers throws open wide the doors to our churches, welcoming caregivers into community.

Though this ministry serves many, there are millions of caregivers, perhaps like you, who have no such resource or are simply unable to get away from their day-in and day-out caring to be part of a support group. If this fits you, we want you to know that you do not walk this journey alone. You are not alone. You are loved and beloved. Your hands are holy; your work is holy. You are a blessing, because in the care you give, you give life, and are building up the Body of Christ.

How to Use This Book

This guided prayer journal was created to help you find the sacred moments and blessings in your caregiving journey. In the pages that follow, you can reconnect with God and find the empathy and gratitude to continue in ministering to your loved one. The prayers and act of journaling will broaden your perspective, giving clarity and insights to strengthen your resolve.

We invite you to make this journal your own, to include your scripture or favorite quotes, to write and doodle, and to express unvarnished truths. You may start at the beginning and move through it day by day, or look over the chapter titles and move directly into a topic that connects with your heart. Use this journal as a tool to open up conversations with the loved one you're caring for, with others, and with yourself. You may find that sharing your reflections with a loved one will help to initiate difficult conversations you've been putting off or that the insights from prayerfully resting in silence with the Lord inspire you to take a new approach when you feel stuck.

Please note that this self-care journal is designed to help you discern and to identify the issues that are most important to you. Because the specifics of each person's situation are unique, you may need to seek the counsel of legal, medical, or financial professionals to address these needs. You can find some resources referenced at the back of this journal or on our Nourish for Caregivers website.

As members of the Body of Christ, we need each other. And in sharing this journal with others, you build Christ's presence here now. We sincerely hope and pray that this book will transform you and your journey into something beautiful that you can carry with you the rest of your life.

ARE YOU
STRUGGLING
TO FIND ENOUGH
TIME?

one

Take One Day at a Time

Give us today our daily bread.

—Matthew 6:11

When you live in survival mode, your mind can become preoccupied with regrets of the past and worries of the future. A daily effort to reframe your life will help you focus on the present moment.

Time is precious. You know that. Yet time can slip away so quickly with frequent distractions and unforeseen situations. Have you ever found yourself wishing there were more than twenty-four hours in a day to get everything done? Does one day blur right into the next? It's quite common to hear a caregiver say, "I live in survival mode most of the time!" or, "I find myself wishing time away while dreading what tomorrow might bring."

Living in this "survival mode" can make it difficult to see the precious moments God gives you in the midst of your caregiving. It isn't possible to literally stop the hands of time. (Time stands still for no one, especially for a family caregiver.) Yet it is entirely possible, with a little practice, to intentionally slow down. And in doing so, you can take in those moments. You can experience the God-given glimpses of precious times spent with loved ones to store away in your memory bank. The secret to finding these special moments is making a conscious effort to live "just for today."

Why only for today? Shouldn't past lessons inform what tomorrow might bring? Don't the responsibilities of caregiving require the skill of anticipation? To a degree, both of these things are true. And yet, too much focus on what was or what will be generates worry, which will rob you of the joy in this present moment.

The reality is there are only three places you can live: the past, the present, or the future. The past is gone. God asks you to leave it behind: "Remember not the events of the past, the things of long ago consider not" (Is 43:18). And the future is also out of your reach; you cannot live there, either. "Do not worry about tomorrow; tomorrow will take care of itself" (Mt 6:34). God goes before you to pave your path.

It is in the present where you meet God. It is filled with all that you need for today. You do not need more hours. You have enough.

THREE KEYS TO LIVING IN THE PRESENT

Shifting your mindset to living "just for today" requires three things: prayer, surrender, and trust.

Prayer is a spiritual gift, one you always have access to anytime, anywhere. In quieting the mind with prayer, you make space to become more aware of the sacred present moment. Science backs this up further, noting that a person's perception of their situation changes through the act of praying. But there is more required of you.

Surrender is a tough one for most everyone. Each of us carries burdens from the past—regrets, resentments, and unmet expectations—that weigh us down and zap our energies. When we ask God for the strength to surrender our burdens and to give us the gift of forgiveness (whether that forgiveness is for someone else or for ourselves), God will help us to let go of the past in order to better focus on the gift of today.

Lastly, *trust* is required to live in the "just-for-today" moments. It calls for you to loosen your control over people and situations and most of all your desire to control God's will for you. Most caregivers think way ahead and believe that they know exactly what others should do, including God. Ever bargained with God? Ever pleaded for a situation to go the way you knew it should go? Turn all these things over to God, who knows far better than anyone, including yourself, what is good for you. Turning both your will and your trust over to God unloads all the clutter that keeps you from focusing on the blessings of living in today.

That's not to say it is easily done. The mind reacts to unknowns by triggering your brain to go to work and try to control what is happening. It is part of human nature. And, as you know, there are many unknowns in the caregiving journey. So many it can become overwhelming at times. Take comfort. You are not alone with these struggles.

Do not become discouraged if your efforts seem to yield little or no results. None of this happens overnight. It is a gradual letting go of what really isn't helping and a slow gain of good that will help. It is ceasing to raise the "what-ifs" and the "what-could-bes" and replacing them with "I've done the best I can today. Tomorrow is another day."

JUST FOR TODAY

> Every believer in this world must be a spark of light, a core of love, life-giving leaven in the mass: and the more he is so, the more he will live, in his innermost depths, in communion with God.
> —Homily of Cardinal Tarcisio Bertone,
> Commemorating Pope John XXIII, 2006

Caring for another person places you on one of the most intimate journeys you can make. Wouldn't you love to spare some of your time each day to just be with your loved one—to be in the moment, to see the good things, and to make the memories that will remain with you forever? Of course you do! We all do. "But how?" you might ask.

St. John XXIII, one of the most influential people of the twentieth century for convening the Second Vatican Council, was known for his ordinary ways. One of the great gifts he gave us is "The Daily Decalogue of Pope John XXIII." The Daily Decalogue offers gentle wisdom to help you embrace a "just-for-today" attitude.

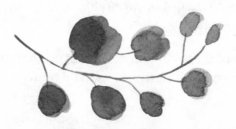

Let's Reflect for a Moment

Here are the highlights of "The Daily Decalogue of Pope John XXIII," which we've summarized in our own words for you:

1. *Just for today,* I will live positively, without trying to solve all my problems at once.

2. *Just for today,* I will not try to improve anyone but myself. I will not criticize anyone.

3. *Just for today,* I will acknowledge I was created to be happy not just in the next life but in this one as well.

4. *Just for today,* I will adapt to others without expecting others to bend to my wishes.

5. *Just for today,* I will find ten minutes to read a good book, to feed my soul.

6. *Just for today,* I will do a good deed and not tell anyone about it.

7. *Just for today,* I will do one thing I do not enjoy doing without drawing attention to it.

8. *Just for today,* I will be on guard against both hastiness and indecision.

9. *Just for today,* I believe that God cares about me as he cares about no one else.

10. *Just for today,* I will not be afraid to enjoy what is beautiful and to believe in goodness.

Which one of these do you need most right now? Today, and every day, give yourself permission to be nourished by God.

Prayer

eavenly Father, be patient with me. It is my nature to want all the answers and to be able to give directions to solve the issues I see today as well as those that could happen. I awaken with worry and go to bed with worry.

Help me to turn to you with all these thoughts that occupy so much of my mind and place them into your hands. Give me the courage, Lord, to truly let these things go and to trust you with them.

May I begin to see the purpose in what I encounter each day. Shield me from worry. Show me how to get comfortable with using all that you give me today wisely, knowing that you already have tomorrow.

Amen.

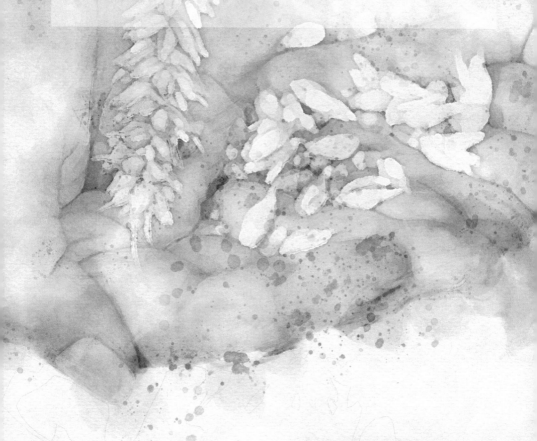

Think about It / Jot It Down

Reflect on your caregiving journey. Quiet yourself. What makes it hard for you to focus on just one day at a time?

Distractions, temperament, and fears and worries are three common obstacles to finding grace in each present moment. Are any of these obstacles for you?

Distractions. Name them. Pray for a moment about how you might eliminate or manage that distraction. Write down your thoughts here.

Temperament. How do you normally see the world around you? Jot down how you are wired. Is your natural temperament helping, or is it an obstacle for you?

Fears and worries. The first step to turning these over to God is to take an honest inventory. Take that step now. What are your fears and worries?

Let's turn now to the most common prayer among Christians, the Lord's Prayer, as found in the Gospel of Matthew:

Our Father in heaven,
hallowed be your name,
your kingdom come,
your will be done,
on earth as it is in heaven.
Give us today our daily bread;
and forgive us our debts,
as we forgive our debtors;
and do not subject us to the final test,
but deliver us from the evil one. (Mt 6:9–13)

Take a moment to slowly pray the Lord's Prayer. Let the words "Give us *today* our daily bread" sink in. Did you ever wonder why God promises just one day's worth of bread? Imagine not wondering or worrying about more than today and trusting God with the rest!

Have **NO ANXIETY** at all, but in everything, by **PRAYER** and petition, with **THANKSGIVING**, make your requests known to **GOD**.

PHILIPPIANS 4:6

Living It Out

FOCUS ON TODAY AND TRUST GOD WITH THE REST

Only you know just how much you are being stretched each and every day. Consider building a new routine for yourself. As you wake each morning, tell yourself, "Today is a gift. I will not get it back. When it is done, it's done. So I am going to place my trust in God and find the gifts that await me in the present moment. I will not get ahead of God. And if I find myself doing just that, I will simply make a note of it and continue to do the best I can."

Be kind to yourself. Prayerfully examine where you are today and what you need. Look again at "The Daily Decalogue of Pope John XXIII." Which of the ten resolutions speaks most to you? Focus on only one. How can you put it into practice? Make a commitment to yourself to live "only for today" and be nourished.

Want to begin each day by reading over this list? Tape a copy to your bathroom mirror as a gentle reminder to live "just for today."

This is the day the LORD has made;
LET US REJOICE in it and be glad.

PSALM 118:24

ARE YOU
STRUGGLING
WITH THE
JUGGLING?

two

REIMAGINE STRESS

Trust God at all times, my people!
Pour out your hearts to God our refuge!

—Psalm 62:9

When stress is often part of your daily reality, it can become too much. By recognizing the signs of unhealthy levels of stress and setting boundaries, you can begin to find relief from the physical, emotional, and spiritual toll it brings.

*C*aregivers are called on to juggle so many things. Some days it may feel like you should be wearing a red rubber nose and clown shoes as you precariously balance family life, health, career, and caregiving! The multidimensional demands can generate a great deal of stress.

Caregiving is rewarding, but it can also be challenging—emotionally, financially, and physically—especially when you need to handle several obligations at once, often with conflicting requirements. No, caregiving is not easy!

How do you cope with stress? Everyone responds to it a bit differently. For some, the demands of caring for a chronically ill spouse, disabled child, or elderly parent is simply a part of daily reality. Others turn to various kinds of coping mechanisms—some healthy, others not so much. Caregivers must never lose sight of the fact that in tending to their own needs in healthy ways, they are better able to care for and be present with those who need them.

A STRESS TEST

How much has stress become a part of your life? Unfortunately, stress will impact your physical and emotional well-being, and if ignored, the effects can be severe. You often don't realize you are distressed until it becomes unbearable. So how do you recognize it sooner? What do you need to pay attention to? Here are a few simple questions to consider.

- *How are you sleeping?* Stress impacts your sleep; you may feel tired but be unable to sleep, or conversely, you wake feeling more exhausted than when you went to bed.

- *How are you feeling? Are you feeling alone, abandoned, or isolated? Do you feel overwhelmed?* Feelings of constant sadness or hopelessness or an increase in crying are signs of stress, which can lead to depression. Be aware that these things can cause you to withdraw, to avoid seeing others, or to avoid participating in activities you once enjoyed. While caregiving can make it difficult to spend time with friends and at other social functions, you still need times of relaxation and enjoyment.

15

- *Are you taking care of your own health? Are you seeing your own doctors regularly?* Sometimes caregivers push off or neglect their own well-being in the busyness of caring for their loved one. And sometimes, too, stress and anxiety can foster poor choices, such as smoking, drinking, or eating in excess. All these behaviors can create or compound existing health problems. On the other hand, eating well and taking time to exercise is important—for your sake, and for the sake of your loved ones.

- *Are you easily upset? Do you find yourself yelling at your loved ones—or even total strangers?* Increased levels of frustration and resentment are signs of stress and manifest themselves in angry outbursts. The inability to deal calmly and efficiently with situations as they arise is a sign of stress.

- *Are you easily distracted or unable to concentrate at home or at work?* When caregiving you can become so focused on your concern for your loved one, or worried about everything that you need to do that it is difficult to concentrate on anything else.

It is important to keep tabs on your stress levels, which will fluctuate. Are you coping well? Or not so well? Recognize too that you need to look at patterns, at the overarching behaviors indicating stress, and seek support.

GOOD STRESS?

Can there be hope with so much stress? Where is there hope? Our hope is in the Lord: "You are my only hope" (Ps 39:8). Jesus is with you every stress-filled step of this journey. In the gospels, Jesus reminds his disciples that his presence, even in times of adversity and distress, is enough: "[Jesus] said to them, 'When I sent you forth without a money bag or a sack or sandals, were you in need of anything?' 'No, nothing,' they replied" (Lk 22:35).

In times of crisis, Jesus' loving kindness is with you. Even when the Lord does not remove your suffering or stress, he is with you. St. Paul tells the Corinthians, and is telling you today, that while he begged the Lord to remove a "thorn in the flesh," the Lord only responded with the reminder, "My grace is sufficient for you, for power is made perfect in weakness" (2 Cor 12:7,9). God's grace is enough for us as well—praise the Lord!

Even stress can be a force for good. Really! "We know that all things work for good for those who love God, who are called according to his purpose" (Rom 8:28). You are called to a purpose; you're doing God's work in caring for your loved one. So remember that stress is a signal. Just as God bestows you with five senses and nerve endings to better perceive if something is too hot to touch, stress can alert you to the need to listen to what is happening and do something, change course, before you suffer harm.

Stress can force you to reset your priorities. When you drift away from God, stop listening to his voice, and attempt to unendingly do more and more, God intervenes—and it's called stress. It helps you stop, pull back, and reconsider your focus. Stress urges you to return to the basics; it serves as a catalyst for change. Even during times of stress, you can collaborate with God's efforts to bring peace, joy, mercy, and charity to others and to yourself. You can realign your priorities, turn back to God, and rely on his providence, trusting he can keep all the plates in the air.

Let's Reflect for a Moment

REFLECTION ON PSALM 23

In the familiar and beloved Psalm 23, God encourages you, offering divine providence, assistance to a better way than stress and anxiety. Notice the specific care—the Good Shepherd leads, restores, guides, and comforts. Prayerfully imagine God taking care of you today. It's your turn to be cared for!

> The Lord is my shepherd;
> > there is nothing I lack.
> In green pastures he makes me lie down;
> > to still waters he leads me;
> > he restores my soul.
> He guides me along right paths
> > for the sake of his name.
> Even though I walk through the valley
> > > of the shadow of death,
> > I will fear no evil, for you are with me;
> > your rod and your staff comfort me.
>
> You set a table before me
> > in front of my enemies;
> You anoint my head with oil;
> > my cup overflows.
> Indeed, goodness and mercy will pursue me
> > all the days of my life;
> I will dwell in the house of the Lord
> > for endless days.

Come and receive all you need! God invites you, honored guest, to his banquet. *Abbondanza!*—such amazing abundance: cleansing and healing; invigorating and refreshing. God generously fills your life with blessings. Oh, you still may walk through dark valleys as caregiving includes difficult, stress-filled days, but you are not alone because God walks alongside, protecting and comforting.

Prayer

You are here with me, Lord Jesus, and you are much bigger than anything this caregiving can throw at me. You assure me your grace is sufficient, and so, Lord, I ask you for that grace, your free and undeserved help. I seek your peace, and I long to find rest in your pasture as I walk along this caregiving path.

I call upon your name, Jesus, to replace my anger with joy, my resentment with compassion, my fears with peace. Enter my days, Lord, bring calm—the deep, absolute, and abiding peace which you alone can give.

Lord Jesus, I look to you and ask for your guidance to help me move beyond my worries and concerns into the person you want me to be, someone who is filled with your peace, your understanding, and your compassion.

Amen.

Think about It / Jot It Down

Though worry and stress can make God feel very far away at times, stress can also cause you to lean harder on God, to depend on him in ways you never have before. What do you need to do to turn your worries and stress into a productive way to draw closer to God?

First, it's important to remember your own care, even as you care for another. How well do you listen to your own body? In what areas do you struggle? Do you have trouble with sleep, concentration, anger? Consider your "stress points," the triggers that set you off. How is the Lord using stress to get your attention, to make a change? Record those promptings here.

Second, recognize not everything in your caregiving journey can be changed; some things happen outside of your control. What are some of those unchangeable areas for you?

It takes courage to recognize and accept those unchangeable pieces. It takes creativity to imagine a response different than the one which causes stress and anxiety.

Consider where you need courage and creativity to prayerfully envision a better situation, a better response, one filled with the Lord's compassion, love, and mercy.

I have **TOLD YOU** this so that you might have **PEACE IN ME**. In the world you will have trouble, but **TAKE COURAGE**, I have **CONQUERED THE WORLD**.

JOHN 16:33

Living It Out

SETTING BOUNDARIES HELPS YOU FIND PEACE

Setting boundaries may not require anything more than a "no" or "not now" response to an expectation put on you. Jesus, for example, set boundaries often, pulling back and carving out space to be alone to pray. You can model his single-minded dedication to center his actions on his heavenly Father's will. How often do you take time to pray? To read scripture? How could you take time to pray more frequently? Ask the Lord to show you how he would like to enter your days.

In addition, ask Mary, his mother, to intercede for you. The Memorare is a popular, centuries-old prayer ideal for times when you really need help. Hold up your stress, worries, and concerns to Mary as you pray the Memorare. Ask for the wisdom and guidance to recognize the need for boundaries and the courage to keep them.

> Remember, O most gracious Virgin Mary, that never was it known that anyone who fled to thy protection, implored thy help, or sought thy intercession, was left unaided. Inspired by this confidence I fly unto thee, O Virgin of virgins, my Mother. To thee do I come, before thee I stand, sinful and sorrowful. O Mother of the Word Incarnate, despise not my petitions, but in thy mercy hear and answer me. Amen.

May the LORD GIVE MIGHT to his people; may the LORD BLESS HIS PEOPLE WITH PEACE!

PSALM 29:11

23

ARE YOU STUCK AT THE
CROSSROADS OF INDECISION?

three

Make Decisions
with Faith

Trust in the LORD with all your heart,
on your own intelligence do not rely;
In all your ways be mindful of him,
and he will make straight your paths.

—Proverbs 3:5–6

When you are living at the crossroads of faith and doubt,
it can be lonely. But you are not alone.

*D*ecisions. Decisions. Decisions. Most people are unprepared for the multitude of decisions that come with caregiving. Many decisions are small and made without much deliberation. Others are very difficult, and some are heart-wrenching. If you haven't already struggled with the doubt that comes with making hard choices, you will. We all do.

At some point, you will find yourself standing at the crossroads of your faith and doubt. Decisions will not only seem unclear; they will also be accompanied with an overwhelming flood of emotions. Many caregivers describe these moments as being in a fog and feeling as if God is nowhere nearby. Have you experienced this feeling? Do you struggle with how to make a wise decision when the challenge seems so great? If so, you are not alone!

Your caregiving journey is unique. Yet you share with other family caregivers similar experiences and choices. Some choices are directly related to caregiving, such as how to maintain a loved one's independence, ensure their safety, select medical treatments, handle end-of-life issues, and so on. There are also tough questions you must answer for yourself and your own family, such as, "Can I continue to work and balance it all with my caregiving?" or, "Can I continue to do this with my own health limitations?"

WHO CAN HELP YOU DECIDE?

In these moments of doubt, lean into your faith. Doubt is not the opposite of faith. It is not. Faith and doubt can exist together; God knows each and every challenge you face. He often uses doubt as a way to help you see your own limitations in order to draw you nearer to him as you pray for answers to your most pressing questions.

What questions do you need answers to? How will you know if the decisions you make are the right ones? Sometimes you simply will not know. This is where faith comes in and prayer becomes very important.

God wants only the best for you and for your loved one. And it is through prayer that communication with God happens. Will the answer be stated out loud and in a booming voice? No, most likely not.

But when prayer is used to seek guidance on choices to be made, something important happens. The decision-making process moves from the head to the heart. Think about those times Jesus went to the mountains to pray for an entire night before making decisions. What he gained, and what you do as well, is the strength and the grace to carry out what comes next.

"FINAL" DECISIONS

Think of decisions as a series of choices to act upon—or not. Initially you may decide not to insist your loved one stop driving, for example. Then, after talking with your siblings and hearing more concerns, you might reconsider and initiate the conversation.

Rarely is a decision final! Let's repeat that: *you can turn back and make a different choice given more time and information.* That is called wisdom, and it removes the pressure of making the one and only perfect decision. The pressure of making a "perfect" decision often leads to paralysis, and making no decision at all is the worst decision you can make.

Still, how do you make a decision when you don't know what to do? Maybe you are too close to see all of the options. Maybe you do not have the expertise needed to make a wise decision. That is true for most of us. It is important to recognize that you do not have to make every decision on your own. You can seek counsel from others, and you can give yourself permission to table some decisions. Not every decision before you needs to be made *right now*!

FIND WISDOM THROUGH SPA MOMENTS

How do you sort it all out? The Bible provides guidance to create a process you can use to make wise decisions. There happen to be a number of biblically based methods that are wonderful, but because caregivers' lives are overflowing with little free time, we encourage you to limit your steps to three: (1) Stop. (2) Pray. (3) Act. In simpler terms, we refer to this as taking a "SPA Moment."

When you *Stop*, you make room for God to enter. "Be still before the LORD; wait for him" (Ps 37:7). It can be a challenge to be still. Locate a space for grace to enter. The size of the space is not as important as the location's ability to allow you to detach. Caregivers often say this requires finding privacy, lighting a candle, or reading scripture for a few minutes.

Then *Pray*. "And we have this confidence in him, that if we ask anything according to his will, he hears us. And if we know that he hears us in regard to whatever we ask, we know that what we have asked him for is ours" (1 Jn 5:14–15). We all pray differently. The important part is to seek God's will rather than seek our personal preferences.

Finally, *Act*. "And whatever you do, in word or in deed, do everything in the name of the Lord Jesus, giving thanks to God the Father through him" (Col 3:17). It takes courage to act. Often, you may have multiple actions you need to take. Realize that taking action may be to gather more information before you make your decision. For example, talk to knowledgeable people, search for information from trustworthy sources, ask for help to review your options, and determine how each option may impact you, your family, and your loved one, considering costs, relationships, and the wishes of the person for whom you are caring.

Especially when there is doubt, fear, and emotions involved in a decision, know that it is often wise to go back and repeat. Take another SPA Moment.

Decisions come and go with nearly every dawning day. Normal everyday life is filled with decisions. As a caregiver, you face some of the hardest decisions one must ever face. Find peace in knowing that Christ's love, strength, and comfort is always available to you.

Let's Reflect for a Moment

Have you thought about calling upon the Holy Spirit for wisdom and guidance? When you invite the Holy Spirit into your life, you are actively seeking the very gifts that are needed to make wise decisions. One of our favorite ways to do this is to reflect on how St. Augustine prayed to the Holy Spirit:

> Breathe into me, Holy Spirit,
>> that my thoughts may all be holy.
> Move in me, Holy Spirit,
>> that my work, too, may be holy.
> Attract my heart, Holy Spirit,
>> that I may love only what is holy.
> Strengthen me, Holy Spirit,
>> that I may defend all that is holy.
> Protect me, Holy Spirit,
>> that I always may be holy.
> Amen.

What line of this prayer jumps out at you? Decisions are part of every caregiver's journey. Prayerfully reflect on your own hard decisions. What do you need from the Holy Spirit this week?

Prayer

*L*ord Jesus,

You walk before me, and you know every decision I will need to make. Yet I feel lost and uncertain at times. There are situations and choices in caring for my loved one that I've never experienced before. I am afraid to make the wrong decision and do not know who to trust to help me.

Jesus, I need you. I ask only for your will to be done. Have mercy on me when I forget to stop and pray before I act. Let me lean on you. Let the Holy Spirit speak to me. I need wisdom that can come only from you.

Show me how to find the courage to scale the mountain of decisions to be made. Accompany me, Lord, too, in the valleys where I feel lost and alone.

As I awaken each morning, I will turn to you, for I know that you will carry me through this journey. Help me to recognize and rejoice in the blessings you reveal to me along the way. For you are always with me.

Amen.

Think about It / Jot It Down

Do you struggle, like so many other caregivers, with thinking you need to make every decision on your own? God does not expect you to carry your burdens alone: "Plans fail when there is no counsel, but they succeed when advisers are many" (Prv 15:22).

Take inventory of the hard decisions you are facing right now. Jot them down. Who could you call upon to help you with these decisions? Think of those you trust and who are good listeners. List them below next to the decisions you've identified. Let the Holy Spirit guide you.

If there isn't anyone in particular who comes to mind, that is okay. Continue to think about it. Especially with the legal, financial, medical, or spiritual decisions you are struggling to make, it may be most helpful to get referrals from others. Ask a friend who may know someone. Or consider asking your pastor to help direct you to a resource. Write a list of the decisions you are trying to make right now, and then write the names of people who might be able to advise you next to each question.

Is there a decision you've been putting off making? Name it here and explore why you've put it off.

Now, take a minute and talk with God about some of the decisions still ahead of you. Prayerfully ask God to help you with overcoming the things that make it so difficult to make these decisions.

Living It Out

LET THE HOLY SPIRIT GUIDE YOU

Take a SPA Moment! Yes, Stop, Pray, then Act. Start by spending five minutes now to Stop and sit quietly with the Lord. Relax as much as you can. Breathe. Feel the presence of the Holy Spirit washing over you. Then Pray about the decisions you face. What do you need most right now? Ask the Holy Spirit for what you need.

Be assured that your needs are heard. Your prayer is lifted up, and God listens to all of your concerns. He may not answer you right away, but know that he is working for your good.

Now find one good thing you can do for yourself. Act on that now. Maybe it is a few more minutes of quiet time. Or perhaps it is taking a walk outside. Find something that nourishes your soul. You deserve this moment of action for your needs to be met so that you can continue to be present to your loved one.

With every decision you face, involve the Holy Spirit!

It is the LORD who goes before you; he WILL BE WITH YOU and WILL NEVER FAIL you or FORSAKE YOU. So DO NOT FEAR or BE DISMAYED.

DEUTERONOMY 31:8

ARE YOU WASTING TIME WISHING FOR THE "PERFECT FAMILY"?

four

FIND PEACE AMID STORMY FAMILY DYNAMICS

Love is patient, love is kind. It is not jealous, [love] is not pompous, it is not inflated, it is not rude, it does not seek its own interests, it is not quick-tempered, it does not brood over injury, it does not rejoice over wrongdoing but rejoices with the truth.

—1 Corinthians 13:4–6

When you look around for help within your family circle, reality may tell you it's going to be difficult. Do not lose hope. You have options.

Have you ever wanted to shout out loud, "Can't we all just get along?" In the good old days, television shows such as *Father Knows Best* or *The Waltons* idealized family life. Even the Great Depression couldn't bring that Walton family down. Millions of people grew up admiring these perfect TV families, making comparisons that too often only set them up for disappointment.

However much you are fascinated by the ideal, there is really no such thing as a perfect family. None of us are perfect. All families experience struggles, disagreements, and failures. It's been that way since the beginning of time! The very first book of the Bible, Genesis, contains story upon story of families who were dysfunctional, at each other's throats, and disobedient to God. Adam and Eve. Noah and his children. Abraham, Sarah, and Hagar. Moses and his siblings. David and his children. Each of them experienced a covenant relationship with God—yet each of their families struggled.

Truly, the perfect family is a myth.

LET'S GET REAL

Accepting the weaknesses and flaws of family members is something you may forget to take into account as you look at the impact of caregiving on your family. Every member of your family has their own style, probably one you admired or disliked all the way back to your or their, in the case of your children, childhood. The stress of the situation can magnify these traits, and you may be stretched to see how what seems to be a "problem" characteristic can be turned into a strength. But it can be done. It does take effort, though.

Caregiving brings with it financial pressure, time demands, and so much more, which in turn puts strain on the inner workings of a family. Even the most harmonious of families feel the tension and have their challenges. Personalities and emotions are amplified, as everyone struggles with how to cope with the changes occurring. In many families, there is an undercurrent of resentment, particularly where one or two are carrying the bulk of the caregiving load. Communications between family members can quickly break down.

Navigating communications and keeping Christ at the center of those communications may just be one of the most important aspects to maintaining peace within the family. Finding gentle and direct words that seek the truth can help preserve familial bonds. Maintaining serenity is everyone's goal, and the most important place to begin is with yourself. When your physical, emotional, and spiritual health are being nurtured, your resiliency is bolstered. From this position, you can find ways to minimize conflict. Continue to feed on the grace and strength that is promised to you from Jesus, who said, "Come to me, all you who labor and are burdened, and I will give you rest" (Mt 11:28).

TIPS FOR SMOOTHER FAMILY INTERACTIONS

Families are made up of individuals, each with their own needs, perspectives, and communication styles. Deep down, everyone wants to feel valued. How well do you understand the needs of others who are involved in the care of your loved one? Do you have insights into how they like to communicate and what works best to avoid confusion or hurt feelings?

Because of each individual's uniqueness, reaching a perfect solution for everyone is impossible. Finding solutions, therefore, requires both being aware of the "land mines" and of a person's weaknesses, as well as making best use of their strengths.

Starting with you: Do you have strong understanding of your strengths and weaknesses? Are there "buttons" people can push that cause you to unravel? We all have them.

You are already armed with many insights. You know your family and their personalities better than anyone else, and you probably have a good handle on what needs to happen in the care of your loved one. Putting all of this information to good use, here are a few ideas for avoiding blowups and seeking resolution:

- *Communicate often.* Set up family meetings, and document agreements made at these meetings. Start each meeting with a prayer to call to mind the presence of Christ.

- *Place issues on the table early*, before there is a crisis. Listen as much as you speak, recognizing some family members who may want to be involved are not certain how to share what is on their mind.

- *Stay focused.* Remember and keep present both the person for whom you are caring and Christ. Place them at the center of every conversation and decision. Christ calls you to act with honor and dignity and to use these two principles as a guide in all you do.

Keep in mind that the one who drives you crazy because they are so detail-oriented could be just the right person to thoroughly manage and ensure tasks are completed. Or the one who desires recognition and is controlling could be great at organizing and achieving results on tough issues. And again, keep in mind, there are no perfect solutions.

WHEN POSSIBLE, PRESERVE THE FAMILY BOND

Jesus, for example, embraced this dichotomy with his own disciples. He knew who among the twelve were more dominant and who were quieter and steadier. Where he saw doubt in Thomas, he knew how to draw out loyalty. Where he saw boldness and temper in Peter, he leveraged those traits to provide solid leadership for the early Church.

So too, you can look at each of your family members, recognize a trait that might seem problematic, and tap into the strength that lies underneath. In seeking to bring out the best in each member of the family, you are tapping into the attributes of love: patience, respect, and truth.

Try as hard as you might to keep the family bonds intact and the lines of communication open, there is no way to control another person or their choices. Recognize what you can do, and also acknowledge what you have absolutely no control over. Calling upon God's mercy and forgiveness is the bedrock of maintaining your serenity.

Recognize that families are fragile and can easily break apart. Keep Christ at the center of all that you do and say. Let love be your guide in how you interact with your family.

Let's Reflect for a Moment

St. Francis of Assisi is known for his love of animals and life of poverty—and for his words about how to be an instrument of peace. The entire premise of this prayer popularly attributed to him is to ask for the strength needed to give of himself in order to meet the needs of others and in turn to bring about peace. Take a moment to offer this prayer slowly, really thinking about where you might be in a position to bring peace to a corner of your world today.

> Lord, make me an instrument of your peace,
> Where there is hatred, let me sow love;
> where there is injury, pardon;
> where there is doubt, faith;
> where there is despair, hope;
> where there is darkness, light;
> where there is sadness, joy;
> O Divine Master, grant that I may not so much seek
>   to be consoled as to console;
> to be understood as to understand;
> to be loved as to love.
> For it is in giving that we receive;
> it is in pardoning that we are pardoned;
> and it is in dying that we are born to eternal life.

Think about your situation and your family. Look at the six suggestions offered in this prayer. For your situation, what do you believe is needed most to bring about peace?

Prayer

$\mathcal{H}$eavenly Father,
Thank you for my family. We are not perfect, and we struggle like all other families. Help us, Lord, especially now, during this time of caring for our loved one. Bring us together and help us to unite. We are bound together by love, but we do not always demonstrate that love well. Give us the ability to recognize in each other what is good, and keep us focused on what truly matters most.

Lord, we lay before you the causes of our tensions and divisiveness. We ask for your mercy and forgiveness. Shine your light upon a path to compassion and understanding among us. May anything that we are hiding from each other be brought forward, and may we not keep a collection of wrongs. Help us, Lord, to seek and find the truth in all things.

Protect us from the snares of sin and evil and help us to be the family you intended us to be. Bring us peace.

Amen.

Think about It / Jot It Down

In one way or another, there is a brokenness in each of us. Nothing you do or say may be able to put your family back together as you wish it could be. What you *can* do, though, is powerful. You can pray.

Pray for the person in your family who is causing you the most distress. How might you pray for them in order to bring about peace?

Now, pray for yourself, and lay before God your needs. In what area of your life do you need peace? Take a few moments to compose the words you would use to ask God.

If you are struggling to feel peaceful or to extend peace to others in what you say or do, Jesus can help you. Ask him to fill you with *his* peace, for you cannot give what you do not have.

The same is true for love. When you feel you cannot love someone, ask Christ to share his love through you. "A new commandment I give to you, that you love one another," Jesus told his disciples. "even as I have loved you, that you also love one another" (Jn 13:34). Are you struggling with this?

Write a little prayer to Jesus, asking him to help you to love someone you find difficult to love right now.

Living It Out

LET PEACE BEGIN WITH YOU

A familiar song about peace says, "Let peace begin with me." Many people quickly jump to thinking this means that the responsibility of creating peace rests squarely on their shoulders, no matter the circumstances. So read the words again. Prayerfully repeat the words. What do you think this phrase means? Are you being asked to create peace for others or to find peace first within you?

At the end of each day, before you fall asleep, examine where you did not feel at peace. Make a note of the specific reason you were feeling that way. Think of one thing you could do tomorrow to start to make peace with yourself.

When you wake in the morning, recall the peace within you that you seek and how you might talk differently to yourself. How might you treat yourself differently?

Even if peace between your family members is slow in coming, if fully ever, can you be at peace? What would that look like for you?

Remember always to be patient and loving with yourself. You can find peace amid challenges when you remember:

In PEACE I will lie down and fall asleep, for you alone, LORD, MAKE ME SECURE.

PSALM 4:9

ARE YOU DOING
THE BEST YOU CAN
BUT FEEL THAT YOU'RE
FALLING SHORT?

five

Balance Wishes and Realities

Love one another with mutual affection; anticipate one another in showing honor.

—Romans 12:10

When walking a tightrope between what everyone wants and what you actually can do, focusing on what is truly honorable for both your loved one and you will help you find balance.

*W*ay back in Catholic grammar school, the fourth commandment was always committed to memory by students: *Honor your father and mother.* This principle from the Old Testament extends to the New Testament, too: St. Paul reminds the early Christians that the fourth commandment is one that comes with a promise, "that it may go well with you and that you may have a long life on earth" (Eph 6:3).

Even in your most rebellious teenage years, the niggling memory of that commandment probably stayed with you, impacting your actions and calling you home. And now, if you are caring for an elderly parent, that commandment to honor surfaces again. Or if you are caring for an ailing spouse or a disabled child, honor still comes into play as you consider how to balance their wishes with your own abilities and needs.

Honor and respect are part of the framework of the Christian faith: Jesus demonstrated in his actions and healings that all people are deserving of dignity and compassion, not merely the rich, the religious, or the already-well. Every human has basic rights: to life, liberty, and happiness, certainly, but also to speech and to be treated without harm or being demeaned.

Consider now what honor and respect look like for a caregiver. How do you recognize the dignity in the person you're caring for? And how do you balance their wishes with what you can or cannot do? Knowing your limits is something every caregiver must eventually come to terms with, one way or another. As you take the time to reflect on your own needs and limits, you can relay them to your loved one in a healthy and helpful manner. In turn, your loved one also has desires and needs to convey. In taking time to listen to their wishes as well as the underlying emotions and concerns, you can find common ground. Conversations then become a two-way street.

Another way to steady the balance is to rely on the Holy Spirit, the Great Helper, God's Spirit of Love, and in so doing, you allow God to work in you and in your caregiving, its daily communications, actions, and interactions. God fills the void, placing his love into the times when balance, honor, and hope seem difficult. This embracing of the Trinity in the midst of caregiving is especially true then as you value and love the people around you whether they deserve it or not. Honoring, then, becomes love in action.

DIFFERENTIATING WISHES AND WANTS

There is a distinction to be made here between honoring someone and honoring their every wish. You are called to honor *the person*. Honor means to regard another with great respect or esteem. It is a choice to recognize the dignity of that person—which is very different from honoring a whim, impulse, or urge that pops up, irrespective of the repercussions to oneself.

Honoring the person can mean expressing your love by listening and asking questions to clarify and understand. You cannot honor someone's wishes unless you know what those are and what they want, in their words. Honor is listening with respect.

Honor is also showing them respect in caring for their needs. Actions in caregiving can help your loved one feel worthy and dignified. Honor can also take the form of showing admiration for the wealth of knowledge and experience elders have. It is visiting and taking time to see them. It may mean listening to "that story" one more time, nodding and chuckling in all the right places. Honor may mean letting your father instruct you on how to run his finances and pay bills, although you've been doing the same for your own household for years. Taking time to listen, again, is showing honor.

PUT LOVING IN THE DOING

Honor does not necessarily mean you must abide by promises made under a different set of circumstances or passively acquiesce when you don't agree with the wishes of your loved one. Nor does it mean you must act against your own morals and values. Remember, blind obedience is not okay. Acting unethical or supporting immoral behavior is not honoring. Sometimes too you may desperately want to fulfill your loved one's wishes but lack the financial, physical, or emotional wherewithal to do so.

Honoring your father and mother means different things in different circumstances, requiring prudential judgment. You are not obligated to move your parents into your home; nowhere does sacred scripture say, "Thou shall not place your parent in a nursing home." In the end, honor comes down to the love you put into your actions. In the words of St. Teresa of Calcutta, "It is not how much you do, but how much love you put into the doing."

How does one show honor? Honor is setting limits and staying calm in the midst of difficult conversations, focusing on the topic at hand and the end goal. Honor is putting aside childhood baggage and avoiding emotional reactions. Honor is not allowing condemning or irrational judgments to cloud the compassion and care you give. Orientate yourself toward your heavenly Father and his wishes, and you will begin to see all other demands fall into place. The Holy Spirit empowers your efforts when you respond with love and dignity to the ones for whom you care. Honor is shown in empathy, gentleness, kindness, and compassion, and as you show these virtues, you mirror the love and mercy the Lord has for all peoples, yourself included.

Let's Reflect for a Moment

ST. HILDEGARD OF BINGEN: HOW EMPATHY AND COMPASSION BRING PEACEFUL RESOLUTION

Saints model faith in action. St. Hildegard, named a Doctor of the Church for her writings and influence, illustrates how the wishes of others do not define who you are or what you can do. She was a remarkable woman—an artist, author, physician, and preacher—yet, at times, was crippled by self-doubt. But in moving from self-reliance to doing God's will, her unique talents became a gift to the Church, reforming and restoring it. She tirelessly engaged her superiors in hard conversations, pursued the truth of Christ, and with love, empathy, and compassion, brought about healing and peaceful solutions.

St. Hildegard wrote about not being able to live in a world defined by others. When caregivers try to balance others' wishes with their own needs, it may feel like the world is being defined by the other. St. Hildegard demonstrates that, although it's difficult and fearful at times, recognizing and naming your own needs sets boundaries and reclaims dignity. God created you to share his love in a way no one else can. You are special, a unique ray of light reflecting his life, truth, and mercy.

Prayerfully rest with the Lord, asking for St. Hildegard to intercede for you.

Prayer

Lord Jesus,

I come to you with my hands wide open, lifted to you. You want only what's best for me, and so, Lord, I hold out my hands to you. Lead me, Lord, as I continue my caregiving journey.

Sometimes I fail to see my own value, my own worth, so I ask you, Jesus, to hold me as the precious beloved child you created me to be. I am wonderfully and fearfully made by you. You know me completely; you know what I can and cannot do. Help me see my limits, where boundaries need to be set, or what is to be surrendered or relinquished. You know what is best.

I put my hand in yours, Lord, to lead me over this mountain. I place myself, my hopes and dreams, into your arms, for I know that all good blessings come from you.

Amen.

Think about It / Jot It Down

What does "honor your father and mother" look like to you? How has how you show honor changed over the years? How does a more robust understanding of honor allow you to consider your loved one's beliefs, needs, and desires as well as your own?

How does this new understanding of what it means to honor a loved one allow you to let go of preconceived notions and assumptions, to put aside knee-jerk responses as well as judging and condemning baggage? Consider how balancing needs and wishes is an invitation to live in the moment, to live in freedom.

Are there any ways you continue to struggle with what it means to "honor" your loved one? Write a prayer, asking the Holy Spirit for wisdom and insight.

Do you think your wishes and your understanding of what you wish for yourself and your loved one have changed over time? How might the wishes of a healthy, middle-aged person be different from those of an ailing, elderly parent?

Have your loved one's wishes changed over time? Write about it here.

Another way of understanding and honoring another's wishes is to reflect on your own. In doing so, you may find ways to better understand the other person's needs and help you prioritize when there are conflicting interests. Examine your needs here.

"I am WITH YOU and will PROTECT YOU wherever YOU GO."

GENESIS 28:15A

Living It Out

HONOR IS A TWO-WAY STREET

Are there wishes that are not negotiable? Why? Show honor by examining the expectations you cannot meet—both current expectations and ones to come. Give yourself permission not to feel guilty. Recognize that you are doing the best you can.

Begin with a prayerful breathing meditation: Breathe in the Lord's love; let it fill your soul and permeate your consciousness.

- Breathe in love; exhale worry.
- Breathe in love; exhale guilt.
- Breathe in love; exhale resentment.

Continue breathing in and exhaling deeply as you offer to the Lord your concerns with an eye toward laying down the challenges and feelings of shortcomings at Jesus' feet.

With a clear mind and a settled conscience, ask the Lord to accompany you as you find a sensitive way to broach the feeling of unrealistic expectations with your loved one. We are called to be honorable in our actions—so do so!

> Likewise, you younger members, be subject to the [elders]. And all of you, clothe yourselves with humility in your dealings with one another, for:
>
> "GOD OPPOSES THE PROUD but bestows favor on the humble."
> So HUMBLE YOURSELVES under the mighty HAND OF GOD, that he may EXALT YOU in due time.
>
> 1 PETER 5:5–6

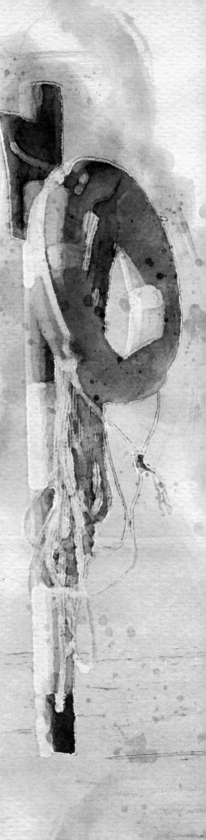

ARE YOU AT
WITS' END
BUT NOT SURE
HOW
TO
ASK
FOR
HELP?

six

Ask and you shall receive

My help comes from the Lord,
the maker of heaven and earth.

—Psalm 121:2

When you realize you cannot do it all alone, it takes courage to seek help. Do it anyway—give others a chance to show their care and concern.

The Morse code emergency signal—SOS—was introduced in 1908 during the height of maritime activity. The set of three dots, three dashes, and three dots quickly became the standard way to attract attention, signal danger, or ask for help. SOS is a palindrome (reads the same forward and backward) and an ambigram (looks the same from upside down), providing an elegant and efficient international signal for distress. There comes a time most caregivers need to send up a flare, a flash for assistance, an emergency beacon before their proverbial *Titanic* sinks. For caregivers, our emergency signal is four-letter word: "Help."

Of course, "help" is a word many of us would rather not use. Whether it's from fear, pride, embarrassment, or concerns about imposing on others, asking for and receiving help isn't easy for most people. And as a caregiver, you may have a misplaced or overactive sense of personal responsibility.

Pause for a moment and reflect on the underlying feelings and concerns surrounding your reluctance to ask for help. It may make you uncomfortable; insecurities or feelings of weakness or failure may surface as you think about needing help. Asking for help requires vulnerability—showing a need that requires another's assistance—and that's not an easy feeling, especially when you're trying to be strong and brave in front of the person you're caring for. Or you may be feeling so isolated you just don't know where to turn.

YOU'RE NOT MEANT TO GO IT ALONE

The reality of caregiving is that no one can do it all alone. Sure, you can try. Very quickly, however, you will most likely be physically, emotionally, and spiritually depleted from trying to shoulder too much. From there, the situation only worsens as you push people away or distance yourself from the help God places before you.

God does not want you to go it alone. You are created for community, to be with others. From the love of the Trinity, you are birthed into a family. At your very core is a need for others. You see it now in the person you care for, the other whose well-being is dependent on you. In the splendid tenth chapter of Luke's gospel, we see Jesus appoint and send out disciples two by two. Not alone. Jesus recognized that his disciples—and this includes you and me—need others to encourage them, minister to them, pray for them, and support them. In community, you can dream, grow, and reach new heights. In communion you can share those dreams and struggles. In fellowship, one person's burden is lessened as others come together to strengthen and lift one another up. Are you beginning to see that an SOS is not only possible but also important?

As you ask for help, you allow others to enter the caregiver journey with you. You allow others to practice works of mercy, giving them an opportunity to grow in virtue and love. Remember how Jesus washed the disciples' feet at the Last Supper (see John 13:1–17), and then he instructed them to do the same? By letting others help you, you allow them to be disciples of Christ who minister, help, and heal. Through their ministrations, you'll experience the comfort and compassion of the loving Lord. By trusting God and trusting others, you deepen your relationships and strengthen your faith.

FOUR Ps OF ASKING FOR HELP

How do you begin to ask for help? Let's look at the four Ps of Caregiver Help.

Pause. Overcome your reluctance. Remember, first, that as you get help, you can better care for your loved one. That's what this is all about isn't it? Also, most people are surprisingly willing to lend a hand and don't think less of you for asking.

Prioritize. Take inventory. Mentally consider your daily tasks, the various parts of caregiving—the ones you like and the ones you don't. Identify what you enjoy doing and what you would be willing to let someone else do. Which tasks are ones only you can do? Where do you find joy or a sense of accomplishment in your caring? What are your most pressing needs, the areas of most concern and worry? Answers to these questions help create your priority.

Plan. Make a plan. In knowing your needs, you can specifically approach someone for assistance or be ready when someone approaches you. Consider others' strengths, whom you might ask for assistance, and how, specifically, you are going to go about doing it. You may need to break large "asks" into smaller tasks that you may be more comfortable delegating. Seek support from church or community organizations. Recognize too that plans fall apart. When they do, don't be discouraged; instead regroup and continue to pause, prioritize, and plan, especially in your prayer with the Lord.

Praise. Express gratitude. Scripture is filled with people who turned to the Lord in times of despair and troubles. Follow their lead. In Psalm 50:15, for example, God reminds his people to "call on me on the day of distress; I will rescue you, and you shall honor me." Do you see the ask? "Call on me." And then what? Praise! The response to answered prayer is honor, praise. So too with people the Lord sends to your aid, thank them. Express gratitude to the friends and family who help, no matter how small. Your "praise" can be as simple as saying thanks, letting them know how your loved one is doing, and remembering them in your prayers.

Pause. Prioritize. Plan. Praise. Jesus reminds us of God's providential nature: "For everyone who asks, receives; and the one who seeks, finds; and to the one who knocks, the door will be opened" (Mt 7:8). Allow God's providential nature to open doors as you ask, seek, and knock. God is always waiting for you, not wanting you to push through your struggles on your own without calling on his grace and compassion. And God's abundance and generosity cannot be outdone! Asking for and graciously receiving help is hard, but you can get comfortable doing so when you realize it is clear in scripture that God wants you to acknowledge your needs.

Let's Reflect for a Moment

Times of illness, hurting, or change are opportunities to encounter God and grow in faith. One particular story from St. Matthew illustrates this spirituality of asking for help: As Jesus passes by, two blind men cry out to Jesus. They first declare faith and trust. Then their acknowledgment and demonstration of receptivity opens the floodgates of God's mercy and love.

> As Jesus passed on from there, two blind men followed [him], crying out, "Son of David, have pity on us!" When he entered the house, the blind men approached him and Jesus said to them, "Do you believe that I can do this?" "Yes, Lord," they said to him. Then he touched their eyes and said, "Let it be done for you according to your faith." And their eyes were opened. (Mt 9:27–30)

Note in this story there are two blind men—again two. You are not meant to go it alone. Prayerfully sit with this reading. Hear the Lord asking, "Do you believe that I can do this?" How do you respond? The blind men boldly proclaimed, "Yes, Lord." Do you? Continue in dialogue with the Lord. Share your needs and be open to "seeing" the response.

Prayer

*L*ord Jesus,

    Sometimes I feel alone, heavy, weighed down by the burdens of caregiving. You know my heart, and I cannot make it without you. So I turn to you. I trust in you.

    I offer you the work of my hands, my daily routine, all I do. You have given me these tasks to do now, and I thank you for this caregiving time. I hold up to you my loved one, and their well-being.

    I thank you, Lord, for the people you place in my life, my family and friends. Help me Lord to see the offers of support, the ways in which they can, and do, extend help to me, especially when I am feeling low and burdened. And help me to remember to turn to you each day for guidance, strength, courage, and resilience.

    Send a hand when I need one, a friendly reminder of your great and grand loving mercy.

    Amen.

Think about It / Jot It Down

If you ask God to help, it means you trust his ability.

You are not a burden; you have been given a burden. And some of these burdens you do indeed need to continue to carry; yet you are not alone in it, for God is always with you.

In the tasks of caregiving that are uniquely yours, you encounter opportunities for grace, opportunities for God to more fully enter your life. How can you offer up to the Lord these needs you have, the burdens you carry?

Can you see yourself growing in grace? How do you see yourself growing in virtue? Ask the Holy Spirit to fill you with grace and virtue.

Think about the person for whom you are caring. Has it been difficult for them to ask for help? What might they be thinking that prevents them from asking for or receiving help?

How might your reflections on asking others for help now influence how you receive requests for help from the person you are caring for? How might these prayerful reflections open dialogue between you?

Living It Out

ASKING FOR AND RECEIVING HELP IS AN ACT OF LOVE

Involving others can be viewed as loving yourself enough to know your own needs and then acting to fill them. Christ commands his followers to love and care for others as they love and care for themselves. To truly care for and love another, you must put the Four Ps into action.

Pause. Remember your focus—caring for your loved one. In accepting help, you can actually care better for your loved one. They will get better care. Period.

Prioritize. What are your top three needs, right now? Determine where you are willing to get help.

Plan. Who and how can you ask? What needs to be put in place to make it a reality?

Praise. Lead with thanks. Thank God ahead of time for the help you will receive. Thank the person as you ask for their help. Thank God for the joy in your caregiving.

So let us CONFIDENTLY APPROACH the throne of GRACE TO RECEIVE MERCY and to find GRACE for TIMELY HELP.

HEBREWS 4:16

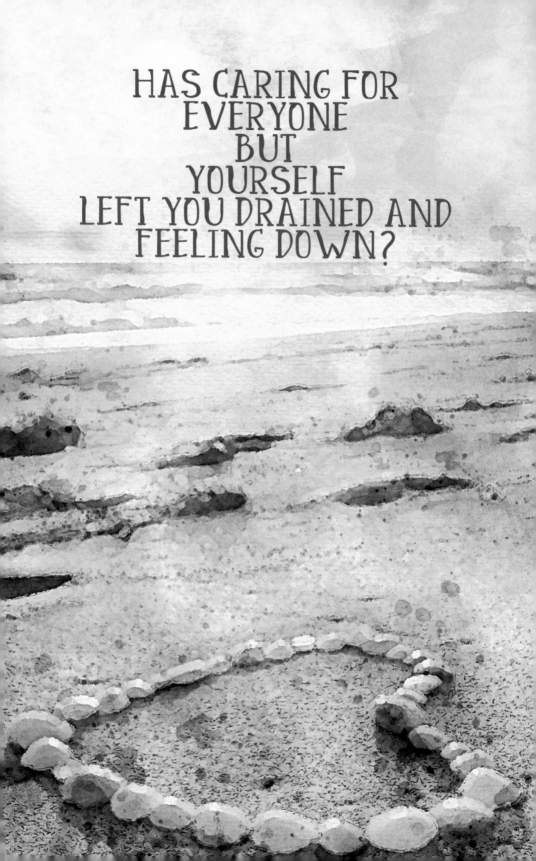

seven

Self-care as an Antidote to Compassion Fatigue

Peace I leave with you; my peace I give to you. Not as the world gives do I give it to you. Do not let your hearts be troubled or afraid.

—John 14:27

When you've reached a low point and find yourself depleted, it's time to make your needs a priority because you simply cannot give what you do not have.

*H*ave you fallen into focusing day-in and day-out on caring for your loved one, only to leave your needs behind? Has it affected your physical, emotional, or spiritual health? You may be feeling exhausted and overwhelmed. You may be snapping at people (including your loved one) or failing to find anything to be grateful about. You may be losing your ability to be empathetic toward your loved one, and as a result, it may be increasingly hard to be empathetic toward yourself.

Emptying yourself to this level is referred to as compassion fatigue. It is a common but significant issue for caregivers. The antidote to compassion fatigue is self-care. Caring for you.

BE KIND TO YOURSELF

Being kind to yourself and taking care of yourself is not selfish! Are you worried about being judged for doing something fun or relaxing? Is it guilt that keeps you from being able to get away to make yourself happy? If so, you are definitely not alone! The vast majority of family caregivers at some point find themselves feeling overwhelmed, exhausted, angry, and even depressed. If it seems like a luxury in which you cannot afford to indulge, realize self-care is actually a necessity.

Compassion fatigue leads to isolation, feeling tired all the time, and a whole host of other health-related issues. When you're giving all you can and running on empty, inner peace is elusive.

Taking time to care for your own needs is the only way to ensure you will have the strength and endurance to give hope, compassion, love, time, and commitment to those you love. But where does "me time" fit in among the sleepless nights, the juggling of too many responsibilities, and the daily grind? Are you beginning to think that feeling whole again is impossible? Just know that there is hope for you, within your reach.

Hope can come from knowing others who've been where you are, who've faced similar demands and yet gave themselves permission to take a time-out. Does anyone come to mind for you? A friend? Another caregiver? Here's someone you may not have considered: Jesus. Yes! Jesus took time away to care for himself when people were demanding more and more of Him. Might he have been looked upon critically for doing so? Possibly. Did that stop him? No.

St. Luke gives a perfect account of Jesus modeling this need for self-care while ministering to the needs of a multitude of others: "The report about him spread all the more, and great crowds assembled to listen to him and to be cured of their ailments, but he would withdraw to deserted places to pray" (Lk 5:15–16). If it is okay for Christ to steal away to rest in the midst of everyone else's needs, then it is okay for you to take time for yourself too.

FACE THE SIGNS OF FATIGUE

Are you thinking, *That's all fine and good, but how can I stop to take care of myself when I'm barely able to keep up with caring for my loved one?* At first, the thought of self-care may seem unrealistic and awkward. You might dismiss the thought as unnecessary. Or maybe you feel anger and resentment at having been unable to take any time for yourself up to this point. All of these are valid feelings.

It is possible to overcome these barriers you believe exist. There is a way, and it resides in the gift of setting priorities and intentions. You must intentionally set out to care for yourself, which begins with acknowledging that changes are happening and becoming laser-focused on addressing them.

What should you look for as possible signs of compassion fatigue? Physically, you may have trouble sleeping or lack motivation to do things you used to enjoy. You might experience headaches or aching shoulders, knees, or feet. Emotionally, you might experience outbursts, harshness toward yourself and others, or feel isolated, depressed, or angry. Spiritually, you might find it harder to forgive others or yourself or find yourself frequently complaining or giving in to negativity. Finally, caregivers often report that, left unchecked, compassion fatigue can erode trust in God until they are no longer grateful for anything and they feel that all faith is lost.

You may not have the ability to see it happening to you. Most of us do not. People who surround you are often the first to provide notice and the external validation that these symptoms are indeed happening. From there, it is up to you to become intentional about making changes to build self-care into your daily life. As with many other goals you've ever set, without a deliberate, conscious effort, it will not happen.

MAKE A SELF-CARE PLAN

What does it mean for a caregiver to be intentional about self-care? There is no universal prescription. Only you know what brings the greatest relief. Here are a few examples that have worked for others, which can serve as a jumping-off point for your own strategies for self-care:

- *Schedule breaks.* Place them on your calendar, then honor them.

- *Set clear boundaries.* Express your needs to others, delineating what you will be doing and what you cannot do.

- *Care for you.* Establish a daily or weekly self-care routine and follow it.

- *Commit to a "Sabbath rest."* The Church in her wisdom reminds us of the importance of rest, as prescribed in the commandment to "Remember the sabbath day" (Ex 20:8). "God's action is the model for human action. If God 'rested and was refreshed' on the seventh day, man too ought to 'rest.' . . . The sabbath brings everyday work to a halt and provides a respite" (CCC 2172).

There's no one-size-fits-all remedy. Let your heart and soul define what you need to do for you. Some examples from caregivers who have their own unique self-care rituals may spark additional ideas for you.

- Grab a cup of coffee or tea and watch the birds; just sit there and stare out the window at God's creation.

- Pick up something nutritious to eat that requires no cooking or cleanup.

- Make a standing date with friends once a week to grab a cup of coffee or walk.

- Get in the car and go to daily Mass once a week—or more if you can.

But what if you just cannot do this for yourself? What if it's gotten to the point where you just can't pull yourself back up? It happens. If this is where you are right now, get a little extra help. Speak with your doctor, a trusted friend, a spiritual director, your pastor, or a therapist.

You are worthy of self-care. You deserve it. God wants this for you and so does your loved one. They can see what is happening to you, which can bring them to sadness, anxiety, and worry for you. But even if no one else can see it but you, God sees.

You are called to care, which includes caring for you as well as your loved one. When you take better care of yourself, you are able to provide better care for your loved one. Too many people drown while helping others not to drown; this does not have to happen to you.

Let's Reflect for a Moment

Constant exhaustion and total self-sacrifice are accepted as just part of the caregiving role. But when the fatigue is relentless and it begins to take a toll on your physical, emotional, and/or spiritual health, it can be of significant concern.

Most caregivers, though, do not recognize the weight of fatigue or its magnitude. Your friends, coworkers, or other family members may see it and tell you they are worried about you. Do you really hear what others observe in you? Do you let it go and carry on, or do you take action to do something about it?

Reflect now on this piece of scripture: "Be doers of the word and not hearers only, deluding yourselves. For if anyone is a hearer of the word and not a doer, he is like a man who looks at his own face in the mirror. He sees himself, then goes off and promptly forgets what he looked like" (Jas 1:22–24).

Take a moment now to observe yourself. Look in the mirror. What do you see? Turn back and look again. See yourself through the eyes of a close friend. Imagine them looking at you right now. What would that friend say to you? How would you respond?

Do not walk away and forget what you see in the mirror. Let it be the motivation to do something to address what you see needs your attention.

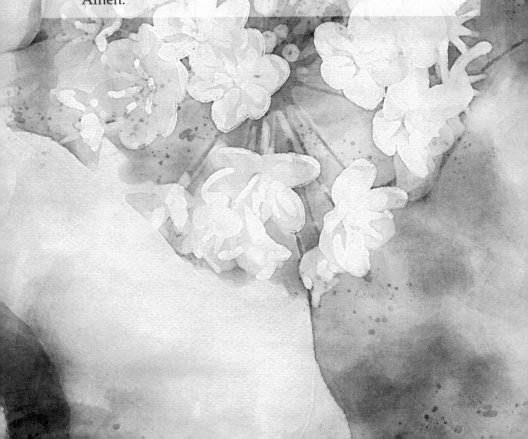

Prayer

Heavenly Father,

Help me see the real me, just as you see me. Make me more aware of my own hurts and needs, the draining of my spirit.

Show me, Lord, how I can start to be just as kind to me as I am to others, especially the one for whom I care. When I feel guilty or unworthy and undeserving of self-love, wrap your loving arms around me and gently cradle me. I need your love to shield me from my tendency to neglect myself.

Guide me in the way I should go. Encourage me to begin to embrace the small things I can do to care better for myself. One step at a time, Lord, with you my spirit is renewed and refreshed. And then, Lord, instill in me a joyful spirit to give compassionately to others and to myself.

In Jesus' name, I pray.

Amen.

Think about It / Jot It Down

Recognizing the reality of what can happen if you do not take care of yourself is the first step toward finding peace and healthier balance in your life. Doing what you've just completed, taking that close look in the mirror, was a huge step forward! Think about it this way: If you turn away and forget what you've seen, your inattentiveness to your needs can directly result in your inability to care for the needs of your loved one. No one wants that to happen.

So prayerfully reflect on how Jesus might coach you. Recall how he practiced self-compassion. He would steal away to get the quiet and the rest he needed so that he could return to caring for others with a heart filled with his Father's peace and love. In his mercy and tender compassion, what would Jesus encourage you to do? What would he say to you?

Look at what you've written. Are these suggestions doable? What, if any, adjustments would you need to make?

In considering what you can do to prevent compassion fatigue from happening to you, what blessings might come as a result of doing these things? How might it change relationships in your life? With your loved one? With others? With yourself? With God?

Living It Out

BE ACUTELY AWARE OF YOUR NEEDS

Create your plan. Set intentional actions to build self-care into your daily life. Remember, less is more! Start by listing three things you can do to care for yourself which take no longer than fifteen minutes. Keep it simple.

Now, pause and pray. Ask God to help you truly be aware of what you need. Let that settle and rest in you. Look again at the three things you've identified and determine which one of these you think would bring you some inner peace. Focus on this one thing, and make a commitment to how you will do this for yourself. You may want to ask someone to hold you accountable and to remind you when you do not follow through on this intention. Ask God for the strength and courage to make this happen for you. You deserve care too!

For I am the LORD, YOUR GOD,
who grasp your RIGHT HAND;
It is I who say to you, DO NOT FEAR,
I WILL HELP YOU.

ISAIAH 41:13

ARE YOU ENCOUNTERING BARRIERS AND BLOCKADES AS YOU TRY TO NAVIGATE A CARE PLAN?

eight

Speak Up!
Find Your Voice as
An Advocate

Whoever confers benefits will be amply enriched,
and whoever refreshes others will be refreshed.

—Proverbs 11:25

When you need practical advice on how to be an effective advocate and caregiver, here are some resources to help you protect life and uphold human dignity.

*Y*ou're accustomed to the day-to-day routine of caregiving; you know the ins and outs of the care your loved one needs. Whether your loved one is residing with you or you are caring from afar, whether it's for an ailing spouse or parent or a child with special needs, you know them best.

For some, the idea of advocacy is a bit unsettling. There are many gray areas in caregiving, and your background or previous experiences may make it difficult to make decisions or take action with confidence. Often advocacy feels like an uphill battle: one more fight you're too exhausted to take on. But it doesn't have to be that way.

WHAT DOES IT MEAN TO BE AN ADVOCATE?

Let's start by looking at the word itself. Being an *advocate* means to support, speak up, plead the cause, or even fight for the rights of another. In the case of a family caregiver, it may mean coordinating with doctors or nurses to arrange care and treatment. It may mean speaking up for a child with special needs in the school system to assure accommodations so your child continues to learn and grow. It may mean having tough conversations to better assure proper care, safe conditions, and protection. For caregivers who are shy or uncertain, advocating can seem an insurmountable obstacle.

However, when you remember to see your loved one as God sees them and recall the sacred identity of all persons, it becomes easier to find your voice and to act with compassion and justice. Faith in Christ imparts an understanding that all life is sacred, every person is precious, and every life is valuable. These foundational beliefs give us the courage to speak and act so as to best protect and respect life and dignity at every stage and in every condition.

This thought is both empowering and sobering, a sacred responsibility. Sometimes emotions get involved, and advocating may not go smoothly, leaving you feeling guilty or hopeless. And yet caregivers must continually work toward greater peace with a commitment to find fair and just solutions.

ADVOCACY IN SCRIPTURE

The importance of an advocate, someone who speaks on another's behalf, is seen throughout scripture. The prophets of old spoke under the authority of God, proclaiming his word and judgment. Jeremiah the prophet, for example, first balked at the Lord's instruction, but he received assurance: "To whomever I send you, you shall go; whatever I command you, you shall speak. Do not be afraid of them, for I am with you" (Jer 1:7b-8a).

You need that reminder too. God is with you!

Jesus also described himself as an advocate, who speaks on our behalf, pleading at the right hand of the Father (see 1 John 2:1). Can you see in Jesus someone who pleads your cause, defends if you go astray, and is with you always? You can trust in the unfathomable abyss of mercy, love, and compassion of Jesus.

Before he returned to heaven after his resurrection, Jesus promised to send his followers an advocate, the Holy Spirit. St. John reassures us we are not alone, for Jesus asked the Father to "give you another Advocate to be with you always" (Jn 14:16).

In the Holy Spirit you can find an advocate who comforts and prays for you:

> The Spirit too comes to the aid of our weakness; for we do not know how to pray as we ought, but the Spirit itself intercedes with inexpressible groanings. And the one who searches hearts knows the intentions of the Spirit, because it intercedes for the holy ones according to God's will. (Rom 8:26–27)

And just as the Holy Spirit groans for you—yes, you are the "holy ones"—so too you are called to protect the dignity, rights, and life of the person for whom you care. You can take courage in the Holy Spirit!

Advocating with a Christ-centered view preserves, respects, and protects the sacred dignity of life from conception to death. Again, as you are grounded in the love of Christ, you can speak up respectfully, recognizing not only the dignity of the person you're caring for but also the dignity of the person to whom you're speaking. Even when you disagree with someone or you need to push until they understand your concerns, you can still do so in a life-affirming manner, filled with charity. It is possible to be respectful and firm.

Take the First Next Step

Advocating requires effort to prepare and plan. If you're caring for an ailing or elderly spouse or parent, begin conversations and listen to their concerns and expectations so that you have an understanding of what their care plan should entail. It also helps you know their preferences for care as well as end-of-life issues. As you care for your child with special needs, advocacy may involve looking at the various options, potential outcomes, and available resources.

An effective advocate helps to find solutions, not just poke holes in plans. Doing homework, finding alternatives, and asking questions all help you recognize the value of each team member who is providing care. Quick web searches are helpful, and the Nourish for Caregivers website also offers links to resources and advocacy groups to aide in these steps.

Advocating also applies to you! All aspects of advocating and being treated with dignity and respect apply to you too.

As you are asserting yourself on behalf of your loved one, realize that it's your voice now that is required to keep them safe, treated well and with dignity. When you're in doubt as to whether to step in and speak up, remember that human life is sacred and all forms of discrimination, mistreatment, and harm are wrong. When you comfort, defend, and pray for another, you are acting as their advocate. Christ calls us and empowers us in our vocational call as caregivers to humbly serve and boldly advocate for the person in our care, mirroring in this world his love and compassion, his justice and mercy.

Let's Reflect for a Moment

THE POWER OF INTERCESSORY PRAYER

Being an advocate includes praying for one another. What area of your caregiving would be strengthened through prayer? To whom could you turn to ask for prayer? Who can pray for you and for your ability to address the issues surrounding caregiving? Oftentimes others cannot do the daily tasks of caregiving, but they can pray.

> Is anyone among you suffering? He should pray. Is any-one in good spirits? He should sing praise. Is anyone among you sick? He should summon the presbyters of the church, and they should pray over him. . . . The fervent prayer of a righteous person is very powerful. Elijah was a human being like us; yet he prayed ear-nestly that it might not rain, and for three years and six months it did not rain upon the land. Then he prayed again, and the sky gave rain and the earth produced its fruit. (Jas 5:13–18)

Have courage! Prayer changes things: the drought in Elijah's time began and ended with prayer! As you pray and advocate for your loved one, the dry period ends and the "earth produce[s] its fruit." Prayer happens in community. Ask others for prayers. And pray yourself. Right now!

Prayer

*H*oly Spirit, the great Advocate,
   Although I'm tired and uncertain, I come to you. Open my eyes, so I may better see the needs of my loved one. Clear my mind, sharpen my intellect, so I may better understand how to respond to their needs. Give me the courage to be like you, the advocate they need, to speak words of life. Help me to bring hope when all seems hopeless, healing when things are broken, and new beginnings when all feels destitute.

   You are the promised Advocate, a helper to be with me always. Come into my days, into my caring, and make them holy. Remove doubts, remove the spirit of cowardice, and fill me with your holy joy, your holy courage. Give me your words. Guide me to know right from wrong, to know your holy, right counsel. Enfold me in your love. Thank you for your presence.

   Amen.

Think about It / Jot It Down

What does being an advocate mean to you? Look again at the earlier definition of the word "advocate"; which aspect resonates with you? Expand on it here.

The voice of a courageous caregiver echoes the voice of God. As you speak up for your loved one, how do you echo the voice of God? How can you better reflect God's love, mercy, and compassion not only to your loved one but also to the people you interact with?

Take a moment: How is the Lord speaking to you about speaking out in love?

Family caregivers advocate best for their loved one by knowing their preferences and understanding their needs. This includes considering potential outcomes. What prevents you from being a strong advocate? What tools or resources do you need? What conversations do you need to have? What steps do you want to put in place to be a voice for them?

Jot down a few of your ideas here.

Think about a specific concern or issue. How could you better prepare for situations or discussions? Where do you need to learn more or ask more questions? What would be a good goal to reach toward?

Brainstorm ideas and record them here.

Living It Out

BE STRENGTHENED AS OTHERS JOIN THEIR VOICE WITH YOURS

> I urge you, [brothers,] by our Lord Jesus Christ and by the love of the Spirit, to join me in the struggle by your prayers to God on my behalf.
>
> —Romans 15:30

You know your loved one and their needs best, but it is not necessary to bear that burden alone. You are part of the Church, and one of the ways the Church lives out its faith is in prayer. God created us to support and pray for one another. As we do so, the Church, the Body of Christ, is strengthened.

So how to go about asking others to "join me in the struggle by your prayers to God on my behalf"? St. Paul did not hesitate to ask for prayer; he knew his ministry was strengthened by the intercessions of others. So too is your caregiving strengthened. Make it a goal to ask someone to pray for you today. Find a praying friend, someone you trust. Or recall someone who previously asked if they could help you. Relay specific needs, but don't worry about every detail or intimate concern. Consider what you need, especially where you feel you continue to be blocked or thwarted in your caregiving. Ask, seek, knock—be a prayer seeker today!

ARE YOU FEELING
FRAGMENTED
AND
DISENGAGED
FROM JUST
ABOUT
EVERYTHING?

nine

Stay Engaged;
Keep Them Engaged

Seek what is above. . . . Think of what is above, not what is on earth.

—Colossians 3:1b–2

When you are having trouble staying focused (or keeping them focused), seek creative ways to be engaged with one another.

*B*eing engaged and fully present in the moment can become challenging for even the most dedicated caregiver; there are simply too many things on the to-do list! As stress mounts or the duties of caregiving become more taxing, it can become difficult to focus, and thoughts can become fragmented. Oftentimes, several different obligations require simultaneous attention, leaving caregivers feeling fatigued and unfulfilled as even the most mundane tasks remain incomplete. It becomes easy to disengage from yourself, your loved one, your family and friends, and God.

GUARD YOUR THOUGHTS

When you distance yourself from God and others, you can begin to feel isolated and alone, as if you're wandering solo in a spiritual desert, focused on some idealized version of the past or future. If you are looking back, you're filled with "could haves" and "should haves." Or if you're unduly preoccupied with the future, you become fearful and worried with "what ifs." God seems to slip away as prayer rituals go by the wayside, and you become preoccupied with planning, problem-solving, or daydreaming. Random negative thoughts, stress, and anxiety mount, and you, consciously or unconsciously, disengage from others.

As mentioned in the first chapter of this journal, God is always in the present, this present moment. And so, because your thoughts drive so many of your actions, parking your attention in the present is critical. Scripture instructs: "With all vigilance guard your heart, for in it are the sources of life" (Prv 4:23).

Your inner thought life, its words and dialogue, matter. Your self-talk can dictate what you do and the way in which you act. Therefore, you need to center your thoughts on God, and "seek what is above" (Col 3:1). It takes effort to guard your thoughts, to choose the pure, holy, and just. St. Paul could very well have been speaking to harried and distracted caregivers today as he did to the Philippians:

> Finally, brothers, whatever is true, whatever is honorable, whatever is just, whatever is pure, whatever is

99

lovely, whatever is gracious, if there is any excellence
and if there is anything worthy of praise, think about
these things. (4:8)

It takes effort to trust in God, to believe that he is with you
in this present moment. But when you think of God and the
things that are honorable, true, just, pure, and lovely, you see
how God is making you a saint and how, as you enter his story,
your circumstances become a part of his plan.

THE GIFT OF MUSIC

One way to see God is in music. Music can touch people in ways
that words cannot. It opens your heart and imagination. Music
is healing, for yourself and the person for whom you care. It is
healing to someone who is isolated or lonely or someone suffering
from memory loss or pain. And music can help you connect with
the sacred and create an opening to encounter Jesus. Music can
help you pray, worship, and honor God.

Music also helps your loved one engage with you and with
the surroundings. It's important to remember that when you feel
distracted and disengaged, so too most likely is the person for
whom you care. In turn, you both pull further apart from each
other; conversations and decisions become strained as does the
time you do have together. But music can provide a bridge to
pull you back together, back into the precious moments that you
share. Music is a simple pleasure; find the delight in the rhythm,
in the gladness you see on the face of your loved one as a familiar
tune is played.

SIX STRATEGIES OF ENGAGEMENT
FOR CAREGIVERS

What are other ways, besides music, that you can use to catch
yourself before you tumble down the rabbit hole of discourage-
ment and distraction? Let's look at six effective strategies for staying engaged.

- *Embrace the world with all your senses.* God has given you five senses to experience the goodness and richness of the world around you. Deliberate attention to bodily sensations brings you back to the present moment.

- *Take joy in simple pleasures.* Share, laugh, touch, breathe, dance, and delight. Move about to more fully interact with the person you're caring for, then use your movement as a reminder of God, who is moving about in your day as well.

- *Accept yourself, including your quirks and limitations.* You don't have to be a perfect caregiver; do the best you can in this particular moment. Treat yourself as you would treat a good friend: with graciousness, forgiveness, and kindness. Forgive yourself and forgive others, and so bridge the divide in relationships. Forgiveness is a deliberate choice to extend to others and to yourself.

- *Frequently readjust and recalibrate.* When you notice the pace speeding up, make a concerted effort to slow down and move more calmly. Modify from multitasking to doing one thing at a time; recent studies are showing that multitasking is not effective and actually decreases productivity. Assess what you need to accomplish, eliminate distractions, and proceed through each individual task. Restart as needed.

- *Settle into the present.* "Do not worry about tomorrow; tomorrow will take care of itself" (Mt 6:34). Just be aware of today, and today's activities. Tomorrow will come.

- *Adopt an attitude of gratitude.* Being grateful is a mindset. Set aside time to thank God, to intentionally review and reflect, which will help you to grow in the conscious awareness of God's generosity and outpouring. Be grateful, too, for the other people who were a part of your day, and extend thanks to them. Find something for which you are grateful.

When you feel dry and worn out, "think of what is above" (Col 3:2). See earthly struggles through the lens of spiritual truths, realizing that the circumstances of the here and now are for the greater glory of God. Trust in God to meet your needs, and seek to hear his voice in your caregiving. As you are fully engaged in your caring for another, you better radiate the love of Christ to them.

Seek the LORD while he MAY BE FOUND.

ISAIAH 55:6

Let's Reflect for a Moment

God reveals himself to you in the people, events, and thoughts of your day. Slow down; take notice. What surprised you today? Where did an unsolicited act of kindness appear recently? Pause to reflect on ways in which you glimpsed God in your day.

Your caregiving is shared with a Lord who walks—no, dances—with you throughout your day. He loves you beyond anything you can grasp, and he wills more for you than you can imagine. You belong to the Lord, and you are his beloved. Let the dance and delight of the Lord in you fill your heart and mind. What does it feel like to be loved by God?

Music connects with the sacred, creating an opening to encounter Jesus as you pray, worship, and honor God in song. Did you know the longest book of the Bible is Psalms? A great big songbook from our loving Lord!

Is music a part of your day? How could you bring more music into your day? How can it connect you to God during your day? Are there certain styles of music that calm or energize you? What about your loved one? Create playlists of songs that inspire you and your loved one.

Prayer

*L*ord Jesus,

My soul yearns for a melody that brings joy and hope and peace into my cluttered, hectic days. I am so worn; my thoughts jump willy-nilly, never settling, skittering from one worry to the next. Preoccupied with caring for another, I give no thought to myself, and sometimes—I'm sorry, Lord—no thought to you. Forgive me; bring me back. Startle me from my preoccupation so that I may listen more carefully; surprise me with a song of your love.

I trust you to lead me into your dance, into your embrace, and into your love, where all my fears are cast aside. You are pure, honest, holy, and true; I cast aside the distractions of the day-to-day, and I think only of you for this moment. With your help, I hold captive my thoughts to rest in you; I settle into your presence and bask in your love. For it is in you that my mind and body and soul is fully engaged.

Amen.

Think about It / Jot It Down

Being engaged takes effort. It takes effort to guard your heart and to choose God. It means you must daily make the decision to take your thoughts captive and "think of what is above" (Col 3:2). Pause a moment. Honestly reflect on your engagement level: Where are you on the inner peace spectrum?

Think about the last couple of days. When were you more engaged? When were moments that you pulled back and only moved mindlessly through your day, without thought to the tasks in front of you? What differentiates one from the other; in other words, can you identify what lead to better engagement?

A variety of factors can affect engagement, including sleep, exercise, a sunny day, level of care needed, or other duties outside of caregiving. List some of your own observations here.

Faith is your response to God. Through Christ you can find life and happiness, even in challenging circumstances. When you become disengaged, how does God call you back?

Record a time when you encountered God in your caregiving.

YOU BELONG TO GOD, children, and YOU HAVE CONQUERED . . . for the ONE WHO IS IN YOU is GREATER than the one who is IN THE WORLD.

1 JOHN 4:4

Living It Out

TAKE YOUR THOUGHTS CAPTIVE

Look again at the Six Strategies of Engagement for Caregivers. Where's the low-hanging fruit in the list below, the first strategy you can easily put in place?

- Embrace the world with all your senses.
- Take joy in simple pleasures.
- Accept yourself, including your quirks and limitations.
- Frequently readjust and recalibrate.
- Settle into the present.
- Adopt an attitude of gratitude.

Plan to enact one strategy today. Jot it down and tape it to your refrigerator. As you open the door, let it be a reminder to you to nourish yourself—grab that low-hanging fruit for better engagement!

For example, take joy in simple pleasures. Hold up your palm. Look at the intricate swirls and whirls. No, look again, really look! God created you; you are wonderfully made. Every line on your hand and every hair on your head is known and counted by God because he loves you.

Allow God's love to bubble into your thoughts and become a prayer today. Let that hand you just looked at so intently be a reminder of God's hand holding you, his mighty arm supporting and strengthening you.

Come, let us SING JOYFULLY
TO THE LORD . . .
Let us come before him with a
SONG OF PRAISE,
Joyfully SING OUT our psalms.
For the LORD is THE GREAT GOD.

PSALM 95:1–3

ARE YOU
EXPERIENCING
CHANGES
THAT FEEL
MORE
LIKE BIG
LOSSES?

ten

SEE THE GAINS IN THE LOSSES

Knowing that affliction produces endurance, and endurance, proven character, and proven character, hope, and hope does not disappoint, because the love of God has been poured out into our hearts through the holy Spirit that has been given to us.

—Romans 5:3–5

When life is changing rapidly, sometimes you have to dig for the blessings. They are there.

hen you hear the word "loss," you might immediately think of death, specifically the death of your loved one. And, yes, that is loss, a big loss that you may eventually experience. However, there are other losses you experience throughout your caregiving journey, most of them coming from personal or circumstantial changes.

Have you ever heard a friend share, "I feel like I'm losing a part of myself," as they talk about their personal challenges as a caregiver? Have you said it yourself? There is no shame in admitting so, because it is a reality based on tangible alterations to your everyday life.

Simply stepping into the role of caring for a loved one represents a change, whether it is having less time for social activities or needing to postpone career plans. Maybe you placed aside hobbies to make room for caregiving. Or perhaps your situation requires you to modify your living arrangements, such as by having your loved one move in with you. Or maybe the change necessitates more travel away from your family to help your loved one. The number and types of changes along the way are too numerous to list. However, over time they start to pile up—some faster than others. And, indeed, it can very much feel as though a part of yourself is lost in the shuffle!

Changes you go through could begin to feel like a giant heap of losses, piling ever higher. Emotionally, the perpetual acclimation is not easy to reconcile. Your emotions can make it harder to open up to see what is happening. After all, many of the occurrences are ambiguous losses, brought about in ways accidental or unintentional. You may not even be fully cognizant of these losses. Regardless, the impact eventually is similar in many ways to the same cycle of grief a person goes through when coping with death.

ACKNOWLEDGING THE GRIEF IN LOSS: FIVE STAGES

Elisabeth Kübler-Ross is famous for identifying the five stages of grief associated with death and dying. You may already be familiar with these stages: denial, anger, bargaining, depression, and acceptance. Today, her theory is also used to describe the stages of grief experienced with losses of all kinds, including the kind a caregiver experiences with the sacrifices and changes required with caring for a loved one.

Although grief is a cycle, not everyone experiences all the stages, nor are these stages necessarily experienced sequentially. Grief is experienced differently from one person to another, and the "cycle" may even loop back on itself—from anger to depression to initial acceptance, then back to anger as new details emerge.

With every change and every loss, you will find yourself adjusting to living a new normal, requiring a great deal of acceptance on your part. As hard as it may seem, keep the faith and keep moving through the cycle of grief. Know that whatever grief looks like for you, there is the promise of it bringing to you eventual healing and growth.

SEEING DIAMONDS IN THE ROCKS

"The LORD gave and the LORD has taken away; blessed be the name of the LORD!" (Jb 1:21). Imagine for a moment that you can squarely look at the pile of losses accumulating like a mound of rocks—misshapen, dull, and gray. These "rocks" are the things that have been taken from you or that you've decided to give up and put aside. Make a mental note of what those losses are for you. Now, pause to consider the other times in your life that you've voluntarily or involuntarily put important parts of your life aside. Maybe those times of putting things aside were not as extensive as in this season of caregiving, but they were losses nonetheless. Because hindsight is 20/20, perhaps you can now see, looking back, where those losses, the unsightly gray rocks, were actually glittering diamonds, blessings in disguise. With the advantage of having moved through these losses and with the passage of time, you may be able to honestly say you are grateful to God for the way in which it all turned out.

That was then, but here you are now, with seemingly more being taken away from you. Is it possible that God is again acting in your life for your good? Is it possible that the inconveniences and sacrifices just might become one of the greatest of all the gifts you end up receiving?

Letting go, though, is not easy, particularly when it feels as if what you are letting go of is a part of yourself. Mentally, you may understand why a change is needed in order to prioritize some aspect of caring for your loved one. You logically understand that loss and change in your caregiving journey are inevitable. Emotionally, though, this realization is often accompanied by fear, sadness, frustration, or anger.

Could the cycles of loss you're experiencing be reshaping you for the better?

Is there something much deeper happening? In scripture God promises, "Therefore, we are not discouraged; rather, although our outer self is wasting away, our inner self is being renewed day by day" (2 Cor 4:16).

Have faith. Blessings will come from these hardships. Perhaps it will be personal growth or becoming more patient and understanding. You may be learning the gift of surrender and gratitude from your loved one. Maybe you've already received the blessing of finding deeper meaning and purpose to your caregiving, or you've been blessed with a deeper relationship with the person for whom you're caring.

Dig deep into your personal pile of losses and the changes you've undergone. Examine them carefully, without judgment. Rearrange them and keep a watchful eye. For the Lord of Light will shine upon them, and it is then you will discover the sparkling diamonds among the rocks.

Let's Reflect for a Moment

Look at your own journey. No doubt there have been disruptions to one or more aspects of your life. Have you struggled with acceptance of these disruptions? Are you still struggling? Resisting?

Anyone who has walked where you are walking now will say that in the midst of those changes which come with caregiving, experiencing feelings of loneliness and abandonment is not only normal but also to be expected. When this happens, recall the beautiful poem "Footprints in the Sand," which concludes with these reassuring words of Jesus: "He whispered, 'My precious child, I love you and will never leave you. Never, ever, during your trials and testings. When you saw only one set of footprints, it was then that I carried you.'"

Imagine Jesus carrying you. Picture it in your mind. How does it make you feel? What signs might you become aware of that confirm times when Jesus has been in the midst of your changes and losses? Was somebody placed in your life to carry you through your fear and struggles? Did you receive an unexpected note or phone call? Be alert. Whether it is today or at some point in the future, you will know just how Jesus has carried you.

Prayer

Dear Lord,
      You know my heart. You know when I am feeling joyful and when I am feeling despair. Please hold me close, especially now, with each and every struggle I am facing. I am trying to deal with the changes in my life during this time of caregiving, but I am not doing well. It is hard for me to accept these changes. Some days I do not recognize myself. I need your love and reassurance.

      Jesus, I know that it may not be your will to remove this hardship and loss from my life, because in the very thing that is causing me pain and sadness you are already preparing to show me the beauty and blessings that are part of it all. Help me, Lord, to find peace and acceptance. Help me to trust you.

      Renew me and help me to discover the blessings you have for me.

      Amen.

Think about It / Jot It Down

Name your losses. Bring them into the light. List all the changes in your life associated with caregiving that feel like a loss to you.

Your losses are tangible. Coping with each of them to arrive at acceptance does not happen overnight. Right now, it may seem impossible. Journaling about your feelings, like you are doing now, is an important step to moving toward that place of acceptance.

Look again at your list of losses. Is there something for which you are grateful now as a result of these things happening? Have you learned something? Has God stretched you in ways that will improve your life going forward?

Saints who've walked this earth struggled, suffered, and intimately knew about losses, just like you and me. St. Elizabeth Ann Seton is one who lost much—sudden financial distress, relocating to another continent to get care for her husband, and the early death of her mother. Yet in an October 7,1805, letter to her own daughter, Cecilia, Elizabeth wrote: "In every disappointment, great or small, let your heart fly directly to your dear Savior, throwing yourself in those arms for refuge against every pain and sorrow. Jesus will never leave you or forsake you."

Close your eyes and imagine flinging yourself into the strong arms of Jesus. Describe the Lord's response to you as you come to him for refuge.

Living It Out

LOSS PROMISES HEALING AND GROWTH

God is closest to the brokenhearted and cares deeply about the loss and grief you experience. One of the most powerful ways to uncover one's gifts is to set out intentionally to be aware of the good you are given each day. Yes, it might feel as if you really are digging for blessings.

Trust that once you get started, it will become easier. Start small. Each morning, as you sip your coffee or stir your tea, make a promise to yourself to find one good thing about your day. Just one. Keep a running list for all those things for which you are grateful. Then, each evening, take five minutes to look at your list and offer your thanks to God.

The LORD is CLOSE to the brokenhearted, saves those whose SPIRIT IS CRUSHED. Many are the troubles of the righteous, but the LORD DELIVERS HIM FROM THEM ALL.

PSALM 34:19–20

eleven

Build a memory bank

What she has done will be told in memory of her.

—Mark 14:9

When overload and exhaustion blur the moments of any given day, all that happens may seem fleeting. Intentionally increasing your awareness and using tools you have at your fingertips will allow you to preserve memories.

The whimsical and wise Dr. Seuss once said, "Sometimes you will never know the value of a moment until it becomes a memory." Any moment can become a memory. The good news is that your caregiving journey is overflowing with moments! The trick is to see them for what they are and capture the ones that really matter to preserve them.

Sometimes life events shape memories; a place, an accomplishment, or an experience stand out. Memories most deeply imprinted in our hearts, however, are the ones that involve people. Whether it is their words, their actions, or simply their presence, the people who pepper our days are often the highlight of our memories.

CAPTURING THE STORY

Memories evolve into stories. Some stories are told and then forgotten. Others live on and are retold over and over again. Think about a favorite story of yours. What makes it special? Most likely, the story calls to mind a feeling or an event, and it brings to life the people at the center of the story. There are often great lessons in a story, both in sharing the experience of hearing the story and shedding light on its meaning. Stories open your heart and mind. Stories are also a way of passing on information from one generation to another.

Did you know that the Bible is the most read book in the world? It is made up of a collection of stories of men and women who struggled to know their God. Imagine if the life of Jesus was not told in the gospels, through the memories of those writers and the inspiration of the Holy Spirit. Thank goodness the words and actions of Jesus were preserved so years and years later his existence would be known as well as his mission and plan for your salvation.

In your caregiving, you have the opportunity to recall and preserve memories that carry great meaning. You also have the ability to create new memories. That's right. In the here and now, with just a little planning, memories can be created for good and shared. Any effort you can make to prompt something special is well worth it: "We must consider how to rouse one another to love and good works" (Heb 10:24).

TIME TO CHERISH: SIX REASONS FOR CREATING LASTING MEMORIES

Have you seen people who, even during the last moments of a loved one's life, gather family at the bedside to take a picture together? Some caregivers spend hours going through old family pictures with a loved one, just to collect the remnants of a memory. Others painstakingly write the details of their loved one's life to share with family and friends—while they are still caring for them!

There are so many beautiful, intentional ways to engage your loved one to create memories. It can give purpose to your day and break up the tedium of caregiving.

Obviously, there are rewards to making the effort and being intentional in transcribing and reproducing stories and memories. Some benefits may just surprise you. Beyond the emotional rewards, there are real health and spiritual benefits associated with creating and recalling memories, which is true not only for you but also for your loved one and other family members.

Here are six ways to create memories while caring for a loved one. Actively engaging him or her can add meaning and purpose to both your lives right now:

1. Creating memories lifts the spirits of both you and your loved one, combating loneliness, anxiety, and depression.

2. It pleases God, who commands us to honor and protect the sense of value and worth of others, especially our parents.

3. It enhances your loved one's quality of life, helping all those involved in their care (their healthcare team as well as other family and friends) to see them as more than their illness or outward physical appearance.

4. It generates happiness in you and others.

5. It produces a lasting legacy that can be shared.

6. It helps you to remember God's blessings in the daily mechanics of caregiving.

Whether you realize it or not, you were called to care by God. And in your role, you have great purpose. Experiencing the moments in your caregiving as something more than the tasks and the doing is absolutely essential. Caregiving and the time with your loved one may just be the most intimate moments you are given to spend together.

PRESERVE THE MOMENTS TO ILLUMINATE THEM LATER

In whatever way works best for you, save and store memories. Make it easy on you. Today, with handheld devices, a quick picture can be taken, a video collected, or notes jotted into an app. Conversations can be recorded.

It does not need to be a big event for a memory to be collected. Simple things such as putting together a jigsaw puzzle and snapping a picture of the finished product or hearing about a favorite recipe as you prepare their meals hold hidden treasures.

Are there memories you want to create? Could you use a little help? Recruit family and friends. One caregiver, whose father served in World War II, asked a neighbor who homeschooled her children if they would like to interview him about the history of the war and his experiences. Using a video camera, the caregiver's family ended up with priceless stories and footage. The possibilities are endless. Just make a plan and carry it out or be prepared to catch special moments when they happen.

Reflect on the experience in your heart. Let it sit there and bring you peace and joy. Our Blessed Mother, Mary, knew the power of moments and memories: "And Mary kept all these things, reflecting on them in her heart" (Lk 2:19). They gave her great peace. In time, they will give you peace, too.

Let's Reflect for a Moment

Building a memory bank requires being aware, watching, and listening. But in all the doing involved in caregiving, you can easily miss a moment to behold. Take, for example, the famous story of Martha and Mary:

> As they continued their journey he entered a village where a woman whose name was Martha welcomed him. She had a sister named Mary [who] sat beside the Lord at his feet listening to him speak. Martha, burdened with much serving, came to him and said, "Lord, do you not care that my sister has left me by myself to do the serving? Tell her to help me." The Lord said to her in reply, "Martha, Martha, you are anxious and worried about many things. There is need of only one thing. Mary has chosen the better part and it will not be taken from her." (Lk 10:38–42)

Caregivers, by nature, tend to be like Martha but secretly desire to be more like Mary. Both Martha and Mary have important roles and are deeply loved by Jesus. What words jump out at you in this story? How do they make you feel?

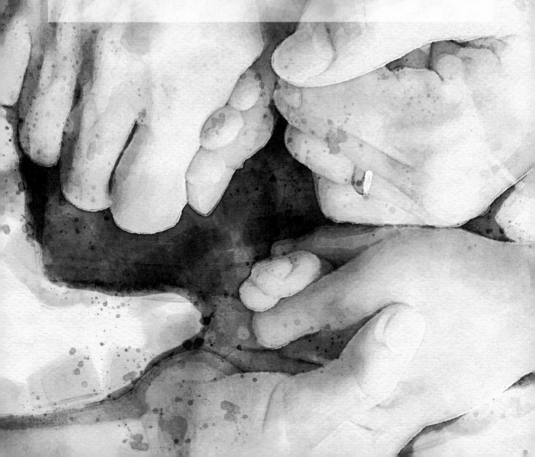

Prayer

Dear Jesus,

Help me to see the time I spend caring for my loved one as a collection of moments filled with meaning and purpose. Especially when I am weary, help me to be aware. Give me the wisdom to know when I need to slow down and remove any guilt I may feel in doing so. Sharpen my senses so that I may be keenly in tune with the magic of the moment.

Illuminate for me the gifts present in my daily caregiving. Show me how to recognize the blessings in the simplest of acts. Help me store away these precious memories of intimacy and love so that I can recall them when I need them most.

May I look back on my caregiving journey as a time of filling myself with the blessings you prepared me to receive.

Amen.

Think about It / Jot It Down

Spend a few minutes now to shine the light on your loved one. Put aside the doing parts of caregiving—meals, transportation, medications, bathing, or whatever it is you have on your to-do list. Focus instead on what you think they cherish most about you. Is it having you there with them? Is it your loving nature? Is it your positive attitude?

Take your time, and write down what you cherish most about your loved one. This may not at first seem obvious to you. People do not often make the effort to say directly what they cherish specifically about another person.

Can you see the blessings they might be receiving from you? What are those?

Now shine a light on your time together. What do you cherish most? Reflect on your experiences today. (Or, if today was a particularly rough day, come back to this later.)

Give yourself the time and space to go deep and explore this one.

For what purpose do you think God has called you to care for your loved one? What have you learned from this caregiving experience so far?

Living It Out

STORE MOMENTS TO CREATE MEMORIES

The value of the moments you are experiencing will only increase as they later become memories. Many things are bound to transpire in your caregiving journey, making it impossible to keep track of them all.

Take a moment now and reflect upon all that you did yesterday—use the space on the previous page if there is room, or use a clean sheet of paper. Write down everything you did, from awakening to retiring for the evening. Now jot down the emotions or moods you experienced throughout the day. Lastly, note how faith played a role in your day.

Can you recall a moment that at first blush seems ordinary yet warms your heart in some way? Maybe it was a touch or a look. Is there a word or conversation you want to remember? What are those things, just from yesterday, that you want to remember? Now preserve those things in whatever way you wish. And consider making this a regular practice!

For where your TREASURE IS, there also WILL YOUR HEART BE.

LUKE 12:34

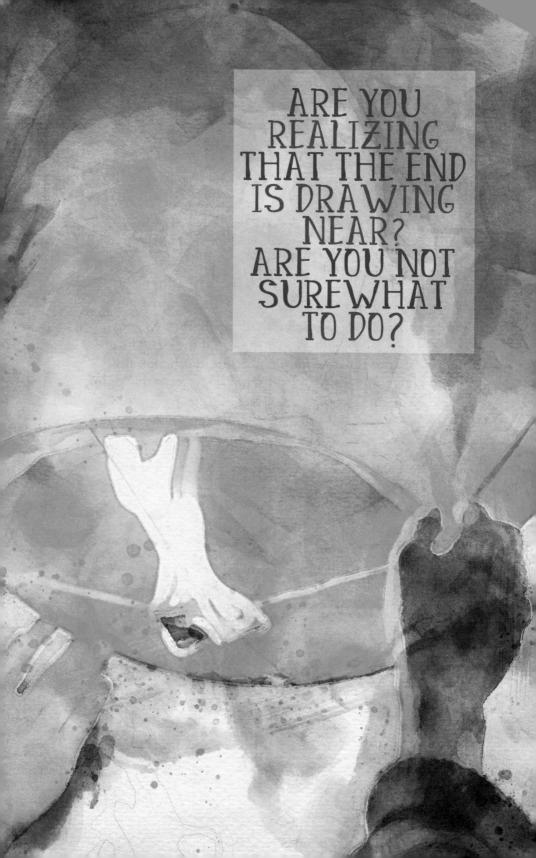

twelve

Moving Toward a Holy Death

For I am convinced that neither death, nor life, nor angels, nor principalities, nor present things, nor future things, nor powers, nor height, nor depth, nor any other creature will be able to separate us from the love of God in Christ Jesus our Lord.

—Romans 8:38–39

When you need to overcome your fear of the unknown and start talking with your loved one about the final chapter of life—death—take comfort in knowing that death is not the final word.

*P*eople don't like to talk about it. Yet, literally, every single person will experience it. Death. It's the talk most often delayed, avoided, skirted around, or glossed over. But as a caregiver, you need to begin to look at death not fearfully but in the spirit of bold preparation; for just as you are a steward of your loved one's life, you also are the steward of their death.

Having frank and honest conversations about death and end-of-life issues is empowering, giving your loved one, and you, the opportunity to express wishes and concerns. It's an opportunity for reconciliation and forgiveness and an opportunity to find contentment in focusing on what really matters. Delaying conversations potentially robs your loved one of the chances to diminish pain and suffering. Knowing their condition and options allows your loved one to make informed, moral decisions. Understanding your loved one's advance directives allows caregivers to make better decisions.

A HOLY DEATH: END-OF-LIFE REALITIES

Numerous recent discoveries in medicine have brought new cures for many diseases, helping people live longer, healthier lives. Yet these advances also complicate patient and caregiver decisions—not only what is physically possible but also what is morally advisable. Just because you can, doesn't mean you should.

Our faith tradition recognizes the gift of life—from conception to natural death—and offers teachings and advice to guide both patients and caregivers so that you can respond with love and compassion during the most difficult and morally challenging times.

Some of the most challenging moral decisions come in those final days and hours. For caregivers, you have a handful of guiding principles:

- All life is a gift from a loving God.

- As stewards of life, we must never directly intend to cause death.

- Dying and well-being can coexist.

Preparing for and addressing issues surrounding the end of life enables you to provide comfort and care; however, it does not mean you need to do everything medically feasible to keep a person alive. When you, as their caregiver, execute their clearly expressed wishes, without trying to change their mind about how they spend the time that remains to them, it preserves their dignity and respects their free will. Allow your faith to be a source of strength and comfort during this difficult time.

In providing comfort and care in your loved one's final days, you create space for the Lord to enter into this time. Dying is more than a medical event. As a caregiver, you can help your loved one move toward a holy death.

SUFFERING AND THE CAREGIVER

Everyone will die, but not everyone has to suffer. Knowing your loved one's wishes, as well as their expectations for care and end of life, is important. It enables you to defer to and enact what they feel is important.

Everyone desires to live well to the very end, and as a caregiver, you certainly want the last stages of life for your loved one to be free of pain and suffering as much as possible. But some of the most challenging moral decisions come in those final days and hours. As your loved one nears this time, they should be given support and allowed to receive the sacraments to prepare for death. Expressing their values, morals, and beliefs is another way in which a person, even as they are dying, can share their faith, demonstrating the holiness and blessedness of life and death.

Life matters to the end of our days here on earth. For all the sadness and suffering that dying entails, faith reminds you that love, hope, gratitude, and joy prevail.

HELP THE DYING ENCOUNTER CHRIST

As a family caregiver, you understand the importance of honor and compassion, and you know all too well the roller coaster of emotions. Fear and doubt are natural and to be expected, both for yourself and for your loved one. But there are things you can do to prepare to best walk with your loved one in their final days. As you discover death is not the final word—for we rejoice in the knowledge of the resurrection—you can move with your loved one to a holy encounter with Christ. But how? How do you practically accept and embrace this notion of holy death?

- *Presence.* Be with them. Be present. Bring your sadness and your sorrow as well as your memories of happier times together. Allow your sadness as well as your joy to radiate to your loved one in your touch, your presence, and your silence. It's okay to cry. It's okay to be yourself. Your presence is the greatest gift you can give your loved one right now; it allows them room to process the changes and transitions they are now going through.

- *Respect.* Pause with your loved one, find beauty in the grace surrounding this moment. Pray—together or silently—and ask the Lord to enter more fully into these moments. Touching a holy medal, crucifix, or rosary beads is a physical reminder of the spiritual. Listen with love, without judgment or contradictions. Minimize distractions and allow your loved one the time and space to speak or be silent. Be grateful for the moment.

- *Awareness.* Watch for nonverbal cues. Minister as you have done, providing comforts and pain management as you can. Your innate compassion and ability to embrace their suffering with sincerity and love will be a calming support during this time of mystery. Be willing to forgive, to see the good in the other, and to relinquish any lingering hurts and bitterness. Your loved one may be wanting your "permission" to die; let them know there is no need to worry or to be concerned for those they are leaving behind. Let the Lord of love enter the space and spread his divine grace.

Jesus is hope during times of transition and change. Death is not the end; it is the beginning. The Nicene Creed professes, "We look for the resurrection of the dead and life of the world to come." This life is not all there is; faith gives the assurance of a life to come—a better life to come. And so, in the final

days, you can look back on the things that bring about a smile, remember what makes your heart sing, and look ahead to joy-filled union with Christ.

Let's Reflect for a Moment

As you gather around your loved one during their final days, don't let any unspoken words linger. Don't let the should-haves, could-haves, and what-ifs build regret and compound sadness.

Is saying "I'm sorry" difficult? Let's face it, there isn't a relationship on this earth that cannot use an "I'm sorry." Forgiveness is freeing and opens the door to communication, reducing guilt and resentment. Forgiveness bears the gift of reconciliation.

The Sacrament of the Anointing of the Sick, sometimes also called Last Rites, includes a secondary effect of receiving forgiveness, since it helps prepare one's soul to meet the Lord face-to-face. Similarly, as death draws near, it is an important time for giving and receiving forgiveness, the person-to-person acknowledgment and articulation of those "last things": both hurts received and inflicted as well as thanks for all the other person has done.

Consider where you may need to extend forgiveness; an "I forgive you" may be needed even before the other asks for forgiveness. It's not always easy, but your first move may be what is needed for healing to progress. Prayerfully ask the Holy Spirit to enter into this hurt.

And behold, I AM WITH YOU ALWAYS, until the END OF THE AGE.

MATTHEW 28:20

Prayer

I need you, Lord Jesus, as I journey with my loved one in their final days. Be with my family as we make these end-of-life decisions that seem truly impossible. Help us to face what makes us sad, find comfort in each other, and find reassurance in your promises.

I pray these defining times are ones that bear witness to you, to your glory and your everlasting goodness. As we go through these hours, I simply fix my eyes on you, assured that you gaze back at me. All doubts flee. Forgiveness and mercy fill my heart and mind. Your peace washes over me.

May my presence bear witness to your tenderness and compassion. Help me to keep you, God, central in the discussions and choices. Fill me with the courage to do what is right.

Thank you for leading me, yesterday, today, and always.

Amen.

Think about It / Jot It Down

"I have no fear of a separation which will unite me with the good God forever," declared St. Thérèse of Lisieux. Death is only the soul leaving its earthly body to be united with God, our Creator who loves us.

Do you struggle with the subject of death? Do you avoid talking about it? If so, why? Why is it difficult to broach the topic of death in your family?

If you have already broached the subject of death with your loved one, good for you! If you have specific questions about end-of-life care, The Nourish for Caregivers website includes end-of-life resources, including state-by-state Advance Directives and End-of-Life Guides. These are not a set of rules or a how-to checklist; rather, they are conclusions drawn from a faith-inspired vision, covering topics such as assisted suicide, life-sustaining treatments, pain medication, nutrition and hydration, and other issues surrounding end-of-life care.

What are the most pressing questions and concerns you have right now?

How can viewing yourself not only as a steward of life but also as a steward of a holy death help you enter into dialogue and discussion more readily? Can you envision what a holy death looks like?

Prayerfully, calmly, bring those images to the Lord, then write your impressions.

Living It Out

RECOGNIZING THE SACREDNESS OF THE JOURNEY

These final moments together can be a time of holiness and healing. "What comes next?" or "What am I supposed to do?" are questions your loved one may be struggling with as they near death. Your lead at this time lends comfort and hope.

The ACTS Prayer Process—Adoration, Contrition, Thanksgiving, and Supplication—is a step-by-step progression that facilitates a movement from thoughts and concerns of this life to preparation to meeting the Lord. The ACTS method of prayer also facilitates dialogue between you and your family:

Adoration. *I love you because . . .*

Contrition. *I'm sorry because . . .*

Thanksgiving. *I'm thankful for you because . . .*

Supplication. *I will be praying because . . .*

Honesty and humility allow space for Jesus Christ to enter into these final days. His grace then accompanies your loved one in a holy death, filled with dignity and compassion.

Finally, don't forget to be kind to yourself. Allow time for grief, for tears to flow. Be gentle to you. You are not alone in your caregiving; Christ has led the way in his sacrifice and triumph over death for our salvation. The Lord be with you.

Even though I walk through the VALLEY of the SHADOW of DEATH, I will FEAR NO EVIL, for you are WITH ME.

PSALM 23:4

Move Forward

It has been an honor to be your companion through this journal and during your caregiving journey. Our prayer for you is continued hope, renewed strength, and the discovery each day of the blessings that God has in store for you. Yes, just for you!

Come back to this journal often. As your journey continues and changes occur, let the wisdom, love, and support found on these pages once again fill your soul. Let the prayers be your companion, available for you anytime, anywhere.

And, if you are so inspired, become a companion to someone else who finds themselves in this role we call caregiver. Share what you've experienced, listen when no one else will, and, together, support each other. In so doing, you bring the light of love and hope of Christ to another.

We would like to share with you additional nourishment and resources to sustain you as you face each new day. Visit our website, www.nourishforcaregivers.com, for free resources, then head on over to our Nourish for Caregivers community on Facebook (@nourishforcaregivers) for daily inspiration and sharing. Lastly, if you would like more individual support from a group of faith-based fellow caregivers, join our private Facebook group called Nourish for Family Caregivers Forum.

Let us leave you with these words:

The SECRET OF HAPPINESS is to live MOMENT BY MOMENT and to THANK GOD for what he is sending us EVERY DAY in HIS GOODNESS.

ST. GIANNA BERETTA MOLLA

MORE RESOURCES TO NOURISH YOUR MIND, BODY, AND SOUL

To support you on your caregiving journey, we recommend the following resources.

WHEN YOU FEEL STRESSED

- Do you know your stress score? Find out at https://nourishforcaregivers.com/caregiver-stress-test/.
- Watch "Coping with Stress and Burnout," from the *Be Nourished* series produced by Shalom World TV, at https://shalomworld.org/show/be-nourished.
- Anxiety and depression can be common symptoms of stress for caregivers. Confidential caregiver-specific self-assessments can be found at https://sagacity.care/questionnaire/gad-7-anxiety-assessment/.
- Are you ready to create a plan that works for you to reduce your stress? Get Nourish for Caregivers' 10-page guide, "A Path to Well-Being," and other helpful resources at https://nourishforcaregivers.com/when-you-feel-stressed/.

WHEN SAFETY IS A CONCERN

- Watch "Keeping Our Loved Ones Safe," from the *Be Nourished* series produced by Shalom World TV, at https://shalomworld.org/show/be-nourished.
- Find videos and tools to support your safety concerns at https://nourishforcaregivers.com/when-safety-is-a-concern/.
- Find home safety assessments, information about hiring workers, and how to get financial assistance to make changes in the home at https://sagacity.care/home-safety-aging-caregivers/.
- Additional support is available in Joy Loverde's *The Complete Eldercare Planner*, available at http://www.elderindustry.com.

WHEN YOU NEED TO NOURISH YOUR SOUL

- Start your day off with receiving Morning Affirmations for Caregivers at https://nourishforcaregivers.com/nourish-morning-affirmations/.
- Find a variety of nourishment for the caregiver's soul at https://nourishforcaregivers.com/when-you-need-to-feed-your-soul/.
- Additional reading (available through Ave Maria Press or Amazon.com):

- ◊ Holy Cross Family Ministries, *Pray with Me Still*
- ◊ Joyce Rupp, *Boundless Compassion*
- ◊ Lisa Hendey, *The Grace of Yes*

WHEN YOU NEED EXTRA HELP

- Find links to national organizations who provide caregiver resources and directories of community services (transportation, food, housing, etc.) at https://nourishforcaregivers.com/when-you-need-extra-help/.
- Scripture as RX is truly medicine for the soul! Meditate upon Scripture with reflection questions and amazing imagery to help you soak it in at https://nourishforcaregivers.com/when-the-medicine-you-need-is-scripture/.
- Additional reading:
  - ◊ Scripture as RX is truly medicine for the soul! Meditate upon Scripture with reflection questions and amazing imagery to help you soak it in at https://nourishforcaregivers.com/when-the-medicine-you-need-is-scripture/
  - ◊ Amy Goyer, AARP National Caregiving Expert, *Juggling Life, Work, and Caregiving*
  - ◊ Virginia Morris, *How to Care for Aging Parents: A One-Stop Resource for All Your Medical, Financial, Housing, and Emotional Issues* 3rd Edition

WHEN YOUR RELATIONSHIPS CHANGE

- Watch "Family Dynamics-The Good, the Bad and the Ugly," from the *Be Nourished* series, at https://shalomworld.org/show/be-nourished.
- Listen to Dr. James Healy talk about "Making Happiness a Habit: 4 Steps to a More Joyful Marriage"; he explores the stresses and strains on relationships and how the habits he recommends are grounded in faith and science: https://rootedinlove.org/Materials/Material/Happiness.
- Read this eight-page guide on how to transform relationships to help your loved one get better care: "Still Me" at https://nourishforcaregivers.com/when-relationships-change/.

WHEN ANTICIPATING OR FACING LOSSES

- Grief occurs both in the small losses that add up along the way, and in the big loss we face as we accompany our loved one at the end of life. Find faith-based videos on dealing with all types of losses and guidance for end-of-life decision making at https://nourishforcaregivers.com/when-anticipating-or-facing-losses/.
- Watch "Finding Grace in Necessary Losses," from the *Be Nourished* series, at https://shalomworld.org/show/be-nourished.
- Additional reading (available through Ave Maria Press or Amazon.com):
  - ◊ Joyce Rupp and Joyce Hutchison, *May I Walk You Home?*
  - ◊ Angela Alaimo O'Donnell, *Mortal Blessings*
  - ◊ Donna MacLeod, *Seasons of Hope Guidebook* and Journals

KELLY JOHNSON is the adult faith-formation director at St. Mary of Gostyn Catholic Church in Downers Grove, Illinois, and the cofounder of Nourish for Caregivers, which seeks to improve the health and spiritual well-being of caregivers. She was an advertising executive until her then-five-year-old son developed a brain tumor, and she cared for him during his illness.

Johnson is a member of the National Association of Catholic Family Life Ministers, the National Conference for Catechetical Leadership, and the Midwest Children's Brain Tumor Center Advisory Board. She is also a member of the Adult Faith Formation Team for the Diocese of Joliet. She earned a bachelor's degree in marketing and English from Loras College in Dubuque, Iowa, and graduated from the lay leadership program from the Institute for Pastoral Studies at the University of Saint Mary of the Lake in Mundelein, Illinois. Along with Debra Kelsey-Davis, Johnson created and hosted a twelve-episode series for caregivers that was broadcast on Shalom World TV.

She lives with her family in the Chicago, Illinois, area.

nourishforcaregivers.com
Facebook: Nourish for Caregivers
Twitter: bjohnson290
Instagram: bjohnson290

DEBRA KELSEY-DAVIS is the caregiver for her aging parents, a registered nurse, and the cofounder of both Nourish for Caregivers—which seeks to improve the health and spiritual wellbeing of caregivers—and Sagacity.Care—which connects patients, family caregivers, and healthcare providers with information they need. Her health-care management leadership spans more than than twenty-five years. Along with Kelly Johnson, Kelsey-Davis created and hosted a twelve-episode series for caregivers that is available through Shalom World TV.

She earned her RN degree at Illinois Central College in Peoria, Illinois, and her bachelor of science degree and master's degree in health services administration from the University of St. Francis in Joliet, Illinois. Certified in lay ministry through the Archdiocese of Chicago's Called and Gifted Program, she has more than twenty years of ministry experience, including catechesis, RCIA preparation, Bible-study and small-group formation, and as a spiritual director for her church's Christ Renews His Parish program. Kelsey-Davis is on the board of directors of the National Association of Catholic Nurses. She lives in the Chicago, Illinois, area with her family.

nourishforcaregivers.com
Facebook: Nourish for Caregivers
Twitter: @DebKelseyDavis
Instagram: debkelseydavis11
LinkedIn: debkelseydavis